A TRUE STORY OF A SINGLE MOTHER

Do you want to buy a copy
of this (or almost any) book?
The library will "special order'
it for you. Ask for details.

A TRUE STORY OF A SINGLE MOTHER

NANCY LEE HALL

SOUTH END PRESS   BOSTON

Library of Congress Card Number: 83-051283

ISBN (paper): 0-89608-208-3
ISBN (cloth): 0-89608-209-1

Cover design by Amy Hoffman & Lydia Sargent

South End Press
302 Columbus Avenue
Boston, MA 02116

This book is dedicated to all the brave single mothers of the world. Their courage is great, for they are scorned by established society, underpaid, overworked, victimized by bureaucratic institutions, and left with few alternatives. They receive no medals. They just keep struggling. And while the male hierarchy is busy creating wars and laying waste to the earth, these powerless women are responsible for providing a wholesome life for our human children.

—Nancy Lee Hall

A special thanks to my editor, Martha McAuliffe, who, from the first "rap group," has unconditionally supported me and listened and listened and listened to all my madness. A true sister to me and all women.

I knew I was in an emergency room in a hospital and that it was the day after the Fourth of July 1980 in San Diego, California. But I didn't know why I was dying.

"I can't get any pulse on the right side of her body," the woman doctor whispered.

"Just help me, please," I moaned.

"We're going to help you," said the nurse.

"Please, please, give me some water. I can't stand being without water. Take me to Lake Tahoe so I can jump in and let the icy water run through my veins."

"Just a sip."

The nurse handed me the glass of melted ice I had carried with me from home.

They lifted me onto a gurney.

Colleen stood beside me, holding my hand. "You're going to be all right, Nancy," she said, her voice trembling. Beautiful auburn-haired, vibrant Colleen, the youngest of my seven children, now grown to twenty-one and doing her best to comfort me.

"Are they going to keep me here?"

"Yes, we're taking you upstairs," said the nurse.

"Goodbye, Colleen. Don't worry. I'll be okay."

"I know you will, Mom."

As I was wheeled away, I blacked out. I don't remember being lifted off the gurney and onto the bed, and I felt nothing when they put the I.V. into my arm. When I came to, I called to a nurse.

"Where am I?"

"It's all right, you're in intensive care." she said.

"What's wrong with me?"

"You're a very sick lady. Try to get some sleep."

She walked away. I still didn't know what was wrong with me. I guessed I really was dying.

My legs, my legs were killing me. I'd have to fight. I didn't want to die. Oh my legs. I couldn't stand the pain. Where was the nurse? Who are all these people with curtains around them? Sick people, all of us sick. I'm fifty-seven years old. I'm probably so old they don't care if I die.

1

And I didn't finish my book. I've got to finish my book! Oh Mother God, don't take me yet. Let me finish my book.

I was afraid to close my eyes. At least with my eyes open, I knew I was alive. I had to get my bearings. I had to be strong and fight. I had always fought and struggled. Who is moaning?

I raised my head a little and saw the center of the room. It looked like a set from Star Trek. All sorts of monitors and desks in a circle. I could see a black man in a white coat and nurses hurrying around. The black man stayed in one spot behind the desks. A big screen over my bed flashed lights. I looked down at the tape on my arm and followed the plastic I.V. tube up to the bottle, slowly dripping, dripping.

The nurse stood over me. "Are you comfortable?"

"My legs." My voice sounded strange and weak. "My legs. Can I have something for pain?"

"I'll get you something."

She came back with some aspirin, and I prayed it would work and take the pain away. It didn't. I didn't want to ask for stronger drugs. I hadn't put any drugs in my body for twenty-one years. Before that I'd had enough drugs, in the form of alcohol, to last a lifetime. As a sober alcoholic, I had a deep aversion to any drugs—they were all poison.

The doctor had said cortisone wasn't a drug. I believed him. He had been annoyed by my questions and feelings about drugs. I felt his annoyance and followed his orders. Had he killed me?

Doctors! Would he have given me more time and care if I were a man? Or some man's wife? There was that place on the financial statement to check "divorced." Most of the time I refused to check it. This time I had, feeling it was a mark against me.

I thought of the children, not children anymore but grown up. They hadn't expected me to get sick so quickly. Neither had I. Their worried faces flash in my mind. Mom was tough. Nothing ever got her down. Now she was down. Just when life was getting easier, coming together. Mother God, help me hold on! I ain't done yet.

THE
RED
HOUSE

I heard a loud knock on the front door. Through the screen, I saw a tall, muscular man in a sheriff's uniform. He did not smile. He handed me an eviction notice, walked back to his green sheriff's car and drove away. I cringed, knowing the neighbors in our nice middle-class neighborhood were watching and curious.

We had three days to vacate the red house Karl had bought us when he retired from the Navy. It was the height of the tourist season in San Diego: June 1961. No one moved in the summertime. The rents were outrageous. How could I find a place for six children, a cat, a dog and myself—a divorced woman with no job? I was scared.

When I'd gone to the lawyer to get a divorce from Karl, I had wanted to be fair. I sat down and figured out to the penny just how much money I needed to take care of the children. I calculated that it would cost about five hundred and seventy-five dollars a month for the house payment, the second mortage, the old bills, food, utilities, dentists and doctors, car repairs, clothes for school, and emergencies. Never mind about my own needs.

Karl was working for I.T.&T. and making good money but I could have asked for two thousand a month, and it wouldn't have made a difference. When Karl felt like sending money, he did. It was never the amount the court had ordered, and most of the time he sent none at all.

I spent what money I got on food, utilities, and other bills, but I wasn't able to make the house payments. When I called my lawyer about the child-support checks that never came, he said, "Please, Nancy, give me permission to garnishee his wages. He owes you twelve hundred and forty dollars."

I recoiled from being that tough. I was Karl's meek "little woman," divorced or not. "I'm sure he'll send it," I told the lawyer, backing off. "After all, he is their father, and he must care." Karl had never been a caring father. Why did I think he would care now? He would only help support his children if the law forced him to.

5

I remembered the day I came home from the lawyer's office with the divorce papers. David got down on his hands and knees and, throwing his arms up and down, said "Thank you, Mother. Thank you, thank you, thank you."

Meanwhile, I had no idea what I was going to do about money for the house or even food. I got up mornings, pulled on my old jeans, and went to the kitchen to make school lunches. Those endless peanut butter sandwiches in brown bags! The three boys were growing so fast. Six gallons of milk could disappear overnight.

"Will you stop drinking that milk from the carton! It's not water, you know!"

"All right, all right."

I knew they were hungry. They were so tall and skinny. I would wake up weekend mornings and hear them fighting in the kitchen over food—rather, no food—and pull the covers over my head until the jungle of noises went out the door.

Never mind about the girls. They seldom made demands.

Colleen had started half days at kindergarten that year. In the morning, she would come to my bed, say, "I'm ready for school, Mom," kiss me goodbye, and leave. I would crawl back under the covers, alone in the house for the first time in years. Alone and afraid.

Mary, my oldest daughter, came home from high school and told me she needed gym clothes or she would get a failing mark. No money had arrived, and things were bleak. I wrote a note to Mary's teacher, promising she would get her gym clothes on the weekend.

I picked up the phone and sent a telegram to Karl, begging for our money. Two days later I got seventy-five dollars, and Mary got her gym clothes. I was so grateful to Karl, I praised him aloud.

"That's sick, Mom," said Mary. "He owes you five hundred."

Mary told me to have faith and to stop worrying, but the problems were coming at me like bullets flying in every direction. The children were going to nice schools where the other children were from stable, settled families. I didn't want my kids ever to be ashamed, and I knew they were struggling to keep up. The schools always assumed there was plenty of money at home.

"My teacher says we have to bring something for the poor kids for the Christmas box."

"I need a costume for the Halloween Carnival. I told my teacher you would bake a cake, will you? All the other mothers are."

"The school pictures are today. They're $2.50."

"Greg brought a turtle for sharing today. What can I take?"

"I need a cape for my part in the class play."

"My teacher wants all the parents to join PTA."

"The nurse said I should have my tonsils out."

"She said I should go to a dentist."

"They're going to make the boys wear suits at our junior high graduation."

"If I don't have a pencil by tomorrow, the teacher says he'll flunk me. The boys keep breaking everybody's pencils for a joke."

"Somebody broke my bike lock. I need a new one."

And there were those awful census cards. One is bad enough, but I had to fill out twelve, two for each child. These cards always left me feeling paranoid. What difference did it make to the school whether I was divorced or jobless? Did that make my children less valuable? Would the kids with influential fathers get the best classes and the best treatment? Did the school think my children were not from a normal home? *Were* they from a normal home?

I answered the phone. It was the school psychologist.

She asked me to please come to school for a conference. I went dutifully and was ushered into her private office and told to have a seat by her desk. She hadn't told me what the problem was, but I knew it wouldn't be good news.

"We've tested three of your children and found that David and Steve will have to go into adjustment classes. Susan will have to go to a special class for slow learners. She isn't really retarded, just slow."

"That can't be," I said. "I don't understand."

"I know it's difficult for you, Mrs. Hall, but I want you to know that we have excellent special classes and Susan will be able to learn better at a slower pace. With children just like her."

Just like her? What did that mean?

I rejected the idea, but I had to believe the psychologist. She was an authority, wasn't she? I put my head down on the desk and cried. She handed me a kleenex. I pulled myself together.

"Why did they wait until she was in third grade to find this out?" I protested. "And what is the matter with my boys?"

"I don't think anyone ever tested them before. Your boys will pick up quickly in an adjustment class and be able to go back to regular classes, but Susan will no doubt be in a special class for a long time."

They'll be labeled too, I thought, cringing. It will always be on the boys' records: adjustment classes. Add that to their being from an ex-Navy, "broken" family. What kind of status would they have in this school system?

"Where is this class for Susan?"

"It's about twenty-five blocks from here, at Crown View Elementary School. She could ride a bike with no problems."

Twenty-five blocks through beach traffic on a bike! Susan was only nine years old.

"Have you told her yet?"

"I feel it is best if you tell her."

I got up and walked out.

She feels it is best! What did she know? Mother God, what would I tell Susan? She didn't even have a bike. She'd have to use one of the boys' and he'd have to walk to school. Even if the old Chevy Karl left us—taking the new Buick— could have made the trip without a reverse gear, I had no money for gas.

I sat in the living room, waiting for Susan to come home from school. The red house was attractive on the outside, but inside, the broken rocker, the lumpy couch with springs barely covered, the worn carpet, the broken tiles on the kitchen sink, and the walls that had more fingerprints than paint on them, punched at the sad fact that I could never get enough money together to fix it all. I felt defeated. And guilty. Guilty about the children, the house, the lack of food, decent clothes, gas for the car to take Susan to a new school. What were we doing in a middle-class neighborhood, in middle-class schools? We were poor people.

Susan came home, and I tried to brighten up.

"You look sad, Mom."

"Come on over here, let's talk. How is school going? Any problems?"

"Well sometimes I can't understand the work."

"How come you never told me?"

"You have enough problems."

"Oh honey, I'll always listen to you." I pulled her near me. "I went to your school today, and they said that after they tested you, they felt you would be happier in a special class. They say this new class will help you learn easier."

Her brown eyes brimmed with tears. "Does that mean I won't be with my friends?"

"You'll make new friends in the new school."

"You mean I have to go to a different school!"

"It's only a few blocks away, and I'll go with you the first few times. Then you can ride David's bike."

9

"Mom, does this mean I'm retarded?"

"No!" I protested, trying to hold back the tears. "It just means you need a little help with your lessons."

"Mom, it's okay. Don't cry. I'll do it."

We hugged and both cried. We both knew it would have to be okay. I felt as if I'd lied to my daughter and done the school's dirty work.

Chris, my eldest, had graduated from high school in 1963. From the time surfing had become popular in California, he had obsessively pursued the sport. How upset I'd gotten when he went surfing instead of doing the yardwork. The tanned bodies, the bleached heads, the wetsuits, and the sand all over the house were a constant. In those days, the sun was shining every day. Later, drugs arrived, and I lived with the darkness of skinny bodies, ratty hair, blank spacy eyes, and death everywhere. Chris was lucky; he escaped drug addiction.

The day Chris left home, I was shocked. A car drove into the driveway with some of his friends in it. Chris yelled at them that he would be right out.

I said, "Where are you going?"

"To Santa Cruz, Mom."

"Santa Cruz!" It was over five hundred miles north.

"Yep, for good."

"Chris! Wait, you can't leave like this!"

"It's better this way, Mom. I have to get out on my own and you have enough to take care of."

I stared at him.

"Mom, it's okay. I'll be fine. I'll write. I love you."

Kids love a clean quick break. Parents need time to prepare for it. I stood there stunned, as the car drove away. I fled to the bedroom and wept. I thought of the times I'd begged him to paint the front screen door and he went surfing instead. Then one day he came home from high school and asked me where the paint was. I looked at him sort of funny but not nearly as funny as he was looking at me.

"What's up?" I grinned.

He just stared at me and said, "Wow, wow!"

"Well, tell me. Don't keep me in suspense."

"And you went through that seven times! Wow! We saw a film on how a baby is born in health education today. I just can't believe you went through that seven times!"

"And now you're going to paint the front screen door?"

He grinned. "Yeah, I though I'd help you out."

Another day, when I had to take Chris to Juvenile Traffic Court for paddling his surfboard in the bay by the hotels, we had a good laugh when Chris said, "Pretty soon my record will be as thick as yours."

My record was from my drinking days. The children's tickets had all been trivial: bicycle tickets, jay-walking tickets, and now this one for paddling a surfboard in the wrong water.

The court gave him a lecture and let him off with a warning.

It seemed odd that I remembered only the warm and endearing times with my children because most of the time I was screaming at them for something they had or had not done. It felt like such a burden, raising the children alone. I felt no one was more isolated in handling life-and-death problems than a single mother.

When Chris said goodbye to me, I watched my first-born drive away to freedom and independence. There was something I had never had the courage to tell him.

I had never told Chris that Karl was not his father.

THE
TROLLEY
STATION

The three days I had to vacate the red house were up, and I hadn't even looked for a place to live. I didn't want to be put out on the street, but I was in a deep depression. All I did was lie on the couch and feel sorry for myself.

Mary ran into the house, excited.

"Come on, Mom. I found us a house. It's really neat!"

Skeptical, I got into our green chevy without a reverse gear, and Mary drove us to Mission Beach. Mission Beach was a four-mile strip of sand, a city block wide. The main street, Mission Boulevard, ran north and south, with the Pacific Ocean on one side and Mission Bay on the other. If you were lucky enough to live facing the bay or ocean, that made you one of the richer inhabitants of Mission Beach. If not, you lived on a court. The courts ran at right angles to the boulevard, and there, people lived in small duplexes, cottages, apartments, and little doll houses that were all strung together like beads on the narrow sidewalks. People of every description lived close together like one huge family.

We walked up to an old gray house located on a court. The front door was open, and a woman was sitting on the arm of the couch just inside the door. I asked her if the house was still for rent.

"Yes, and I'm really mad. I've been waiting for some tourists from Arizona for two days and they haven't showed up. They were going to be my summer rentals. I get so tired of tourists. They pay the rent and think it's a license to wreck my place. I guess everyone on the beach has the same problem. When they leave, it costs me a fortune to fix it up again."

"I'd like to rent it on a year-round basis," I said.

She paused to consider. "Well, why not? How about one hundred and thirty dollars a month, year round?"

Suddenly I remembered I only had ten dollars left to my name.

"Could I give you a ten dollar deposit until tomorrow?"

"Fine with me. Do you have your own furniture?"

"Yes, I do."

"Then I'll take this stuff out of here tomorrow."

I quickly gave her the ten dollars before she changed her mind, and she wrote me a receipt. I told her I had six children, a dog, and a cat, and she didn't even blink. Mission Beach was like that—then.

The house was an antique, formerly a trolley station that dated back to 1860. It had been refurbished many times, and during the time we lived there, many old-timers from the Beach stopped by to tell me stories about the house and the old days.

There were three bedrooms, a very large living room with a stone fireplace, and an old garage out in back that had been made into a beach shack. Perfect for the boys. The fireplace had handcarved scenes of historical sites in San Diego. It was a unique house.

We lived on the Bay side of the boulevard, but the Pacific Ocean was only a hundred yards away. Every evening I walked to the ocean to watch the bright sun disappear into the water. I could sense the turning of the earth. In the winter, it was even more spectacular. Mother God picked up her paint brushes, dipped them in pinks, purples, reds and blues, and went mad painting the sky. My poverty was less grinding when I lived with that kind of beauty.

The day we put down the ten-dollar deposit on the trolley station, however, I couldn't relate to Mary's enthusiasm. I had nothing left—not our first month's rent or even the night's groceries. I juggled and plotted. No one I knew could lend me that much money. I had nothing to sell. My only hope was Karl, and I prayed he would send some of the money he owed us.

The next morning, Karl's check for two hundred dollars was in the mail. I spent years living this crazy financial nightmare. I guessed all poor people did the same. There was no alternative.

Two neighbor men helped us move into the beach house where we were to begin our new life. I still had no idea how we were going to survive. My depression subsided, mainly because I was so busy trying to get us settled.

After everyone found their way to the new schools, I had the phone hooked up, the gas and lights turned on, and spent my last few dollars on groceries. I sat on the old couch, with the springs working their way through the threadbare covering, and took stock. I knew my ass was up against the wall. I had no family to turn to, except my brother who lived in Buffalo and had his own life struggles. My mother had died, my father had died, my stepfather had died, my grandparents and aunts and uncles had all died. I alone was responsible for six lives. I hadn't worked in twenty years. I wasn't trained for anything. I had done some drafting work during World War II, but I was positive I had forgotten how to do it. I was great at diapers, but there wasn't much call for a diaper washer.

All the years I was drunk—the years when the children were small—I staggered around the house proclaiming that I was going to write the Great American Novel. Not only did I not write, I didn't even read. I couldn't focus long enough. I never dreamed that sober, I could do anything I chose to do—even write a novel.

At the beach, I wrote at night when all the children were asleep. I sent out plays and short stories and accumulated a pile of rejection slips. I knew I could never support my family by writing.

I needed money and I needed it fast. A friend of mine told me about baby-sitting jobs at the large hotels and motels in San Diego. She was making extra money that way. I called and left my name with several hotels. Almost immediately I received a call from the nearby Sea Hotel. I drove the old car, parked it alongside the Cadillacs, and found the room where my first job waited.

I knocked and an eastern Indian man opened the door. His wife was standing behind him, dressed in traditional Indian clothes, a red circle in the middle of her forehead. Only the man spoke English. They were going out to dinner. The two children were good and went quietly to bed at the designated time. I watched TV until the parents came home, and he gave me ten dollars for a three-hour stay. I was happy that I had finally made some money on my own, and the next day we ate again. That summer I made about five hundred dollars.

The problem was, I had to be available night and day. When a call came, I had to leave or miss the job. Mary helped me with the other children, and I learned to be more comfortable with the idea of leaving my home to work. Being brought up in the traditional way, I always feared something terrible would happen if I went away, like the house would burn down. I felt I would be punished for leaving the children, even to go to work. Especially to go to work.

Finally I began taking my notebook with me and writing in the motel rooms while I watched the little rich kids sleep. I looked at their expensive things, especially the shoes lined up under the suitcases. Oxfords, patent-leathers— shoes for every occasion. My kids had one pair of shoes each, a beat-up pair of sneakers for play, school, and Sunday church.

The motel jobs were my first encounter with the super rich who vacationed in California. The clothes, the cars, and the money they threw around boggled my mind. Oil people from Texas, ranchers from Wyoming, bankers and businessmen from the East Coast, and many rich people from other countries. I took their money with glee, and I'm sure they wouldn't even remember what I looked like. I could have been Ma Barker, kidnapping their children for ransom, for all they knew. They never asked for references or credentials. They dumped their children on me and went out to play.

After the tourist season was over, I began to work more steadily on my writing, finishing a one-act play and working on an autobiographical novel.

The same friend who told me about the baby-sitting jobs kept yelling at me on the phone to go for job interviews. I couldn't argue with her because she was divorced, had eight children, and was working. But I was afraid.

"All my stockings have runs in them."

"So go with runs in your stockings!" she screamed.

"But who's going to watch my kids?"

"They'll be fine. Just go get a job."

She gave me her strength when I had none of my own. I spent most of my time worrying without taking any action. I felt helpless. My face broke out in a rash that spread to the rest of my body, and when it cleared up I knew I had to earn real money. My lawyer friend spoke to someone at a ship-building company, and I was scheduled for an interview.

I couldn't hold my hand steady when I filled out the application. My mind flashed back to when I had been a good draftsperson, but it had been long ago, with a lot of pain and dying in between. I lost my confidence. I applied for the job of engineering aide instead of draftsperson. Way down at the bottom of the application, it read "Other positions held." I wrote in tiny letters: draftsman.

They told me to report to work on Monday as an engineering aide, which was a fancy title for a file clerk. My starting salary was seventy-two dollars a week, and when I received my first paycheck, I saw that after taxes, I would take home fifty-nine dollars.

The first day was horrendous. I was frightened and didn't have the slightest idea of how to deal with people in an office situation. I wasn't even sure I could file the blueprints correctly. I had also forgotten that engineering offices are powered by men. The few women I saw were file clerks, secretaries and mail "girls."

I soon got into the ritual of working. Every morning, I ran through the dirty shipyard, racing to get to the engineering building on time. I was never sure the old car would make it. I had trouble finding clothes to wear because I didn't have many. At night I sewed up ripped blouses, tried to polish my old shoes, and wondered if I could afford a few new things when I got paid.

Every night after work, when I sprawled on the couch exhausted, the children asked for something they needed. Shoes, paper, pencils, notebooks. Mary was a senior and needed a formal for the Senior Prom, $25 for a class ring, and $5 for a cap and gown.

I wanted to scream, "Why in hell do you need a class ring or a formal?" But, damn it, she deserved something.

Once I overheard Steve bawling out his five-year-old sister. "Hey Colleen, don't tell people we had cereal for supper."

"Why not?" she asked innocently.

"Because I said so."

I kept plodding. We scraped by, and the children seemed happy. They were becoming self-reliant and learning to help one another. Colleen stayed with a next-door neighbor after kindergarten until Mary came home at three in the afternoon. Susan and the boys looked after themselves. Susan appeared settled in the special class and had made a friend or two in the neighborhood. The boys spent most of their time at the beach.

At first I worried all day at work, thinking about the children. Later I was able to put them out of my mind on the job. But there were always emergencies.

Mary called at work. "Steve just fell on a picket fence, and there's a hole in his forehead."

"I'll be right there. Put a rag on it until I get home."

I rushed out of the building, ran across the shipyard, and drove home as fast as I dared to take Steve to the hospital. They stitched up his head and wrote me out a bill for forty dollars.

Because I could not depend on my paycheck alone, I still depended on Karl to send money. I was receiving some money from him every month, but one month I got nothing. I was finally angry, and I told my lawyer to go ahead and garnishee his wages. In three days I got a check for twelve hundred and forty dollars. It wasn't all he owed us, but it was a windfall. I immediately paid past due bills, paid back people I had borrowed money from, and went out to buy a new car. I put five hundred down on a Rambler station wagon.

The payments were seventy dollars a month. I took a risk that I would be able to make the payments and have decent transportation to go to work. And the car went in reverse.

I drove home and got all the kids, and we went for a long ride. We were all laughing and having a good time. We rode up to the mountains and, on the way back, stopped for ice cream cones.

"How are you going to make the payments if Dad doesn't send us any money again?" Tim asked.

"I don't know, Tim, but I will. I have faith. We're going to be okay."

For the next few months, Karl sent the correct amount ordered by the court: $575. What a relief. I was able to buy all of us decent clothes and shoes and even put a little in the bank. But then the checks stopped again. I guess he thought he was safe and no one was paying attention. I ended up using my savings and being back where we were before.

One day at work, the boss came up to me and said, "I see by your application that you once did some drafting. Would you like to go on the board again?"

I froze. From somewhere inside, a weak voice answered yes.

I picked up the first drafting pencil I'd held in twenty years, and it felt as though I'd never left the drawing board. After a week, I got a raise to eighty dollars which meant that if I didn't get Karl's child-support money, I could at least pay the rent, car payment, and grocery bills. It felt great to be independent.

I worked harder than ever, keeping the family functioning. Writing at night was my private world, something I did for me alone. No one else could touch that. I kept sending out my favorite one-act play, *Lost*. It was rejected twenty times. I finally put it in my desk drawer, thinking my writing days were over, but I continued to write anyway. Depression and elation were a part of my nature, and I could get out of a depression almost instantly through small signs from my Higher Power, whom I call Mother God.

Just at the right moment, Susan would say, "Come on, Mom, don't give up now."

Or Colleen would open the refrigerator and exclaim, "Oh good, we're poor again."

When we were running low on money, the children would help by baby-sitting, washing cars, and mowing lawns. Then they'd hand over their money to me. At those times, the fighting stopped, and the house reeled with love.

Suddenly, I couldn't find the energy to write at night. I managed to get to work every day, but the depression I was in was almost immobilizing me. At night, I simply sat.

I knew from six years of sobriety that I'd better get to an AA meeting and be with my people. I did not want to drink, but I could see no hope of ever being able to support

22

my family in a decent manner, and the problems seemed insurmountable. However, we were surviving, and my raise had made us independent for the first time. Why was I feeling empty?

In the three years I had been divorced from Karl, I had not the inclination or the time to think about love or sex. I masturbated a lot without thinking I needed a man. I didn't trust any man.

When I walked into the AA meeting, everyone said hello to me, but my depression was swallowing me up. I saw the same faces, the same set-up I'd seen for six years. As I sat listening to each speaker, I thought, this is garbage, all this happiness, thinking all our problems are miraculously solved just because we're sober. I felt like a woman from another planet.

I had a very bad attitude.

As the meeting progressed, however, I began to feel better. The subject was depression, and I heard exactly what I needed to hear. I got a second wind.

At the very end of the meeting, a man stood up and asked to speak. He was your classic tall, dark, and handsome.

"I've decided to stay sober for ninety days," he announced. "I hope I can do it."

Eyes popped, people grumbled, and I moved a little to get a better look at this man who defied all AA philosophy. AA suggests that you stay sober only a day at a time. In truth, it works. But I couldn't help chuckling. I always did like rebellious people.

After the meeting, I walked up and introduced myself. "Do you come to this meeting often," I asked.

"I guess I'll be coming for at least ninety days."

Under the laughter, I was struggling with powerful feelings, an unexpected and overwhelming attraction to the man. Was I blushing? Were those beads of sweat on my forehead? People were walking around us, talking and laughing, and my heart was pounding so hard I had to leave.

"Well," I stammered. "I hope to see you next week."

We stood there staring at each other.

"I'll be here," he said.

I walked to my car, feeling giddy, and drove away. I was forty-one, I told myself. So why was I suddenly turned on by this stranger after so many years? And I had so many problems already, I didn't need to complicate my life with a man. My head tried to reason, but deep down I knew I wasn't going to use my head this time. I wanted love.

I couldn't get to sleep that night. I tossed and rolled and felt like a cat in heat.

The following Sunday night, I returned to the meeting and this time, I was prepared. I had bought a new pink sweater that I knew I looked good in with my long dark hair. It was the first piece of clothing I'd bought myself since I divorced Karl.

He wasn't there. I went back every Sunday night for three months and didn't see him. It was disappointing but not depressing. I was getting a lot of strength from the AA meetings, as always, and gradually moved away from the hope of seeing him or any man who would want a woman with six children.

I began looking over the men at work. They didn't excite me at all. I returned to my writing and became completely engrossed in my book, believing again that it might pay off and I would be able to get the family out of our semi-poverty.

I was sending my manuscripts to publishers and getting rejections with harsh comments about the plays and stories.

One letter said: "We're sorry we don't have a market for this type of story." And at the end: "When you're playing a losing game maybe you should change the game."

I wondered why anyone would try to discourage a beginning writer and for the first time I thought it might be because I was a woman. I considered using a man's name. But I wasn't a man and I liked my name.

Many times I cried. Some of the criticism was valid and I learned to sift through it and accept what I believed to be true.

One Tuesday evening I fell into another depression. To fight it, I rushed out and mailed some more manuscripts.

After I dropped six brown envelopes in the mailbox, I stopped at the supermarket to buy some things for supper. As I was checking out, I glanced at the fourth person in line behind me. It was him.

"Hello," I gulped, accepting the change the clerk put in my hand.

His face lit up. He's glad to see me, I thought. "How are you, Nancy?"

"Fine." The second customer in line pushed by me. I couldn't leave, and I couldn't just stand there spouting chit-chat. "I'll wait outside for you."

I stood outside the supermarket, my bag of groceries shaking in my arms. He came out, carrying a pair of rubber gloves he'd just bought.

He touched my arm. "I'm really glad to see you."

"I haven't seen you at the Beach meeting lately."

"I've been away," he said. "Have you been going Sunday nights?"

"Occasionally," I lied. "How did the ninety days go?"

"Great. You ever go to the La Jolla meetings Tuesday night?"

"Sometimes."

"Are you going tonight?"

My mind went crazy. I wanted time to get myself under control, to get ready, so I said no.

"Well, would you give me a ride Sunday? I'm staying with my mother temporarily, and I don't have a car."

"Sure, I'd be glad to. Where do you live?"

He wrote down the address on a scrap of my grocery sack. He lived about three blocks from my house. We decided to meet at eight, and we both knew that gave us an hour together before the meeting. I watched him walk away, feeling like a balloon floating up, up, up and out of sight. I walked into the house singing. Mary looked up from her homework.

"I think I'm in love," I announced.

She laughed. "Oh? That's nice."

"Don't tell anybody yet."

"I won't, Mom."

I asked Mary if she would stay home with the children Sunday night. She had been the mother of the family all the years I was drinking and was tired of the baby-sitting role, but she was dating and having good times on the weekends, so she agreed.

I wore my pink sweater, and Duke was standing out in front of his house, waiting for me. He smiled as the car pulled up. He looked good, rugged and handsome.

The body chemistry was electric as he sat beside me in the car. We spent our hour before the meeting in the coffee shop, looking at each other across the table.

He reached out and touched my hair while we waited for coffee. I was going crazy.

"You working?" I could barely talk.

"For a contractor, setting tile. I'm just living with my mother temporarily."

That was twice he had told me. I wasn't suspicious.

"I'm a draftsman," I said. "For Ace Shipbuilding."

"Divorced?"

"Yes."

"Do you have kids?"

"Seven," I nodded.

"Seven! Hey that's a lot of kids."

"That's what I think."

We laughed. I was so glad to have passed the hurdle, I never thought to ask about his husbandhood or parenthood. Besides, I was mesmerized by his deep-set brown eyes.

All my sober life I had prayed to find another sober person. I had had enough drunkenness and violence. I was excited about finding someone who was sober and in AA. I fantasized about going to meetings together and having a true bonding of spirits.

During the meeting, we sat at a long table with about twenty-five other people. I hardly heard a word anyone said. Sitting so close to Duke, I couldn't stop thinking about touching him, feeling his arms around me, making everything okay. I was so nervous and wanted him so much the sweat appeared on my face. I felt everyone must know what was happening to me and prayed they wouldn't call on me.

I drove us home and parked in front of his mother's house. We talked a while; then Duke finally moved toward me. He put his arms around me and we kissed like I'd never been kissed before. I felt as though I were home again. Maybe he did too.

"I'm a very lonely man, Nancy."

"I'm lonely too," I told him.

And later, "Will I see you tomorrow night?"

"If you want to."

I gave him my phone number, and he said he would call me when he got home from work. I was so nervous I wanted him to get out of the car so I could go home. He kissed me again and got out.

On the way home, I thought about the children, what they would say. Mary would understand. But what was there to understand? I hadn't done anything. Everybody needs to be loved.

The kids were in front of the TV watching and eating sunflower seeds.

"Okay, it's ten-thirty. To bed."

"Just 'til the program's over, Mom. Come on."

"Okay, but then to bed."

I went into the bathroom and looked in the mirror. God, I'm alive again!

The next morning I went to work, and they informed me that the work had slowed down and I was to be laid off at the end of the following week. I didn't care because I was in love. I thought it would be nice to collect unemployment and rest for a while, maybe work harder on my book and plays.

That evening, as soon as I stepped into the house, the phone rang. It was Duke. We talked about our workdays, and I told him I was being laid off.

"Be sure to sign up for unemployment right away," he said, "so you don't have to wait for your money."

We made arrangements to go out that night—in my car, of course. I quickly fixed hamburgers for supper, told Mary I had a date, and jumped into the shower. Mary offered to sit again.

As soon as Duke got in the car, he said, "Let's go up to the top of the hill and park."

We looked out over all of San Diego: the lights, Mission Bay, and the Pacific. I wasn't too interested in the view and neither was Duke. We grabbed each other.

Finally he said, "Don't you think we're a little too old for this? Why don't we go to a motel?"

We pulled into a second-rate motel called "The West-ward Bound." He got out and rented the room. I sat in the car, petrified. He sensed my nervousness and kept his arm around me while we were going to the room. It was only minutes before we were both naked in bed.

I got my training from the movies and books of the 40's, and was playing the passive role. Duke was the typical aggressive male. The first time, he ejaculated almost immediately, and I was frustrated but didn't show it. We talked and then fucked again, and it was better. On the third try, I finally reached orgasm and felt satisfied.

The stories he told me that night were beyond belief, and I was fascinated by his weird ways. In one sense, he was very old-fashioned, but every story was more spell-binding than the last, and I was all ears.

The reason I hadn't seen him for three months was that he had been in an honor camp, serving an old sentence for being drunk. He had been arrested ninety-eight times in his life for being drunk. Once in Arizona, he had been handcuffed to three Indians and thrown into jail. He'd been run out of a small town in New Mexico.

He had been in the Navy and seen action in the Pacific. When he got out, he developed a phobia about his ears being too big and wouldn't go out of the house without a hat. After six years, he had them operated on.

His family had been very poor, and his father had been in prison. As a kid, he had been shifted around to the different relatives and had fought every kid in town because of the things they said about his father. In the ninth grade, he dropped out of school and had never gone back. He had worked at laboring jobs, including plumbing, tile-setting, and cement mixing.

His father had been an alcoholic but had died of a heart attack after being sober for seven years. His mother now ran a rest home for old women. He had two sisters and a brother.

If these stories of Duke's life weren't enough to hook me, the wound clear through his stomach and out his back was. He wouldn't explain it. Later I found out he had been in an alcoholic ward, screwing the nurse, when her boyfriend came in and knifed him.

That night I thought, this poor man, he's been through hell. I'm going to make his life beautiful from now on.

I called home at midnight. "I'm having such a good time, Mary. Is it all right if I stay all night?"

"Sure, Mom. The kids are all sleeping and everything's fine. You deserve a good time, so don't worry and have fun."

For the next three weeks, I was on a grand and glorious fantasy trip with Duke. He was sweet talkin' and knew how to make me feel like the most beautiful, sexy, perfect woman he'd ever met. Once in a while he'd add: "You're pretty smart too."

No man had ever said those things to me. Karl had spent nineteen years berating and beating me into submission. I had responded by being constantly drunk. But those days were behind me forever, and now I was blissfully in love.

We didn't have money for a motel every night, so we fucked every place we could park: in lots, at the beach, in the park—always in the back seat of my car.

One night, when we were going at it, a policeman shined his light in on us.

"Oh...okay," he said and left while Duke was desperately pulling up his pants. We laughed all the way home.

Introducing Duke to my children wasn't easy for me. I felt guilty and expected the children to disapprove. I finally did it, I suppose, because I wanted Duke in my bed and the house forever.

We found all six of the children at home. I presented Duke as though he were a prize. The girls were polite. The boys said hello and took off for the beach. Nobody was impressed very much, but I couldn't wait to get the children's opinions the next day after school.

"Well, what do you think of Duke?"

"He's big enough," said Steve. "Bigger than Dad."

"Yeah," said Tim. "He's probably just another jerk who'll end up beating us up for twelve more years."

I was shocked. "Duke would never hurt you! Or even touch you."

"It's okay," Tim shrugged. "I'm going to practice guitar now."

"Please, Tim, just give him a chance," I told his retreating back.

"He seems nice," said Colleen.

"Listen, Mom," said Mary, "if you like him, it's okay with us." And later, when we were alone, she added: "I heard you screwing on the couch springs. Why don't you use the bed?"

From that point on, Duke spent the nights with me in my bed, and the children accepted him as a fact of life.

During those days my reality was standing in long lines at the unemployment office to collect my fifty-five dollars a week. Duke was working but never gave me any money. He bought food once in a while because he loved to eat. So did the kids. I saw quickly that I had taken on another child, but Duke was a new kid who fit in easily with the others.

Then one morning after he had left for work and I was getting the children off to school, the phone rang. It was Duke.

"Can you meet me at the Red Barn for a cup of coffee?" His voice was low and shaky. "Right now."

"Is something wrong, Duke?"

"I'll tell you when you get here."

I left the kids and drove to the Red Barn. I saw Duke sitting inside. He came out to the car.

"What's wrong, Duke?"

"Come on inside." Duke was walking as though he were watching a movie on the sidewalk. I had never seen him so depressed. I was sure he was going to tell me someone died.

"Now, will you tell me! What's going on?"

"You'll have to drive me downtown. I have to turn myself in. I have to go back and do more time at the honor camp on an old drunk charge."

My heart was pounding. "I thought you served your time!"

"I did, but I got drunk when I got out, and the fuckers caught me again. There's no way out unless I run, and that's useless."

"But you've been sober a couple of months."

"They don't give a shit. They got nothing better to do than pick up drunks."

I was crying. We hung onto each other and when I looked up, Duke was crying too.

"They can't do this to us," I protested. "Why are they doing this? Why?" I was getting hysterical. "We'll run, Duke. We have to! Let's do it." Never mind the children. I couldn't face losing him. I couldn't stand loneliness again. What is logic in the face of passion?

I pulled myself together. "When do you have to go?"

"Right now. Or they'll come looking for me."

In the car, we kissed and held on to each other. Duke told me to start the car. "I'll be in the County Jail for a while. You can come see me on Sunday."

"I will, Duke," I blubbered. "You know I will."

"Will you write me?"

"Every day. I'll write to you every day."

"I'll write to you too. Every day."

In front of the Court House, I stopped in the no-parking zone. "Well, I got to go, doll. I love you. Keep your legs crossed."

We clung together for a moment and he got out. I drove away looking back, wondering what I was going to do without him. When I got home, all I could do was sit on the couch and cry. I flashed back to the hundreds of times I had waited on the couch, crying, for Karl.

The children started coming home from school and saw I was upset. I told them Duke had had to go away for a while, and they went about their business, not overly concerned.

My fantasy world had collapsed, and I was definitely back in reality. Play time was over.

During my drinking days, I had spent a night in jail once, but I had no idea what the set-up was for visiting. Sunday the waiting room was filled with the relatives of prisoners. I was the only white person there. Our names were announced one by one over the loud speaker when it was time for our visits.

"Visitor for Duke Ellsworth."

I moved cautiously to the darkened room and sat down in front of a thick glass divider. The guard brought Duke to a chair on the other side. Duke picked up a phone and motioned me to pick up mine.

"Hi, sweetie, how are you?"

"Are you okay, Duke?"

"I guess. Chow time makes me mad. The damn niggers take all the meat out of the stew, and by the time it gets to me, it's soup."

33

"Don't start a fight, Duke, talking like that."

"Well, it's the truth, babe."

"Is everything else okay?"

"This will be the last time I'll be able to see you here. They're shipping me out to camp tomorrow."

"How far away is that?"

"About sixty-five miles. I'll send you a map of how to get there. Will you come visit me?"

"Sure, honey."

There I was, looking cow-eyed through the glass, talking on a telephone to my lover, a man who was definitely something other than what I had invented for my absurd fantasy. I felt as though I were in the middle of a Bogart-Lupino movie. It didn't matter. Nothing mattered except blind obedience to my sexual desires and therefore to Duke.

I don't know how long we talked, but true to the movies, the guard came up to Duke and said, "Time's up, Duke."

The traffic was heavy on the way home, and the tears were trickling down my cheeks. I didn't see the car in front of me and had to pull my wheel quickly to miss it. That brought me to.

What was going on with me? How could I drive sixty-five miles up to the mountains to visit Duke? I had no money for gas. I had no job. I had to take care of my family.

For the next few days, I had a hollow feeling in my stomach and couldn't eat. It subsided, and I bought the morning paper to look for a job. A civil engineer had an ad in the paper for a draftsman who could ink. I phoned, and they told me to send my resume. I made several copies of my resume and sent one to them and others to marine engineering companies. I decided to wait a week and then start calling them.

In the interim, I had Mary's high school graduation to worry about. Graduations were costly. Senior pictures, class ring, rental of a cap and gown, a new dress to wear under the gown, new shoes. Earlier in the semester, Mary had worked at Woolworth's for a dollar ten an hour after school and had saved thirty-two dollars for a dress for the Senior Prom. For her graduation, I wanted to pay for everything. Together we made it.

The sun beat down on the bleachers set up on the football field. All the parents—fathers as well as mothers— were there in their best clothes. I felt eyes on us when the five children and I trooped in and searched for a space on the bleachers.

Colleen stood up and spoke out, "Where's Mary, Mom?"

I still felt nervous about the watching eyes. "Shhhhh, you'll see her in a minute, honey."

The school band started playing "Pomp and Circumstance" and the senior class came marching out onto the field. We spotted Mary, and I got a lump in my throat. I was proud of her. She had made it. Two down and five to go, I thought.

The graduates sat, and the principal got up to speak. The microphone went off. Confusion and bustling. It came back on, and the principal made a little joke. A minister gave the invocation, something about God watching over these graduates as they took their first steps out into the world.

Mother God, I added, watch over Mary now and always. Help her keep her spirit of independence and confidence. And let me find the money to help her go on to junior college in the fall as she plans. She deserves an education and a chance in life.

The speeches were long and dull. They dragged on and on, patriotism, freedom of choice, hard work and moving up, and the glorious system that offered Fame and Fortune to everyone. Go forth, graduates, and make us proud.

Go for welfare and unemployment, I thought. I saw Mary squirming on the metal chair and wondered if she too were thinking, oh sure, hard work and moving nowhere. Dollars scrounged from God knows where. Freedom of choice to struggle endlessly or to end it all. But this was my second graduation ceremony. I didn't expect anything better.

When the two hundred graduates got up to get their diplomas and Mary walked across the stage, I choked up again. Her brothers and sisters cheered, yelling for all they were worth, and I let them.

At the reception afterwards, Mary introduced me to some of her friends' parents. They were pleasant enough, but I felt like the old woman in the shoe. I called to the boys, who were wrestling on the lawn, and we all went home to the trolley station.

Duke wrote me a letter as soon as he got to the honor camp. I wrote back immediately. He asked me to go visit his mother. He said he had told her all about me.

One day, having been out to look for a job and being dressed better than usual, I decided to stop by and meet her. The green and white duplex was spotless. The lawn looked as though each blade of grass had been cut separately, and the rose garden was so perfect it looked artificial. There wasn't a weed anywhere around the yard.

I knocked on the front door and Mrs. Ellsworth, Duke's mother, answered.

"Hi, I'm Nancy."

"Oh. Come in." She had a soft voice.

She was tall, had gray hair, and was wearing glasses. She reminded me of my childhood Sunday School teachers. She had no make-up on but looked neat and trim as the lawn.

"Come into the kitchen and we'll have a cup of coffee."

"That would be nice," I said.

Everything in the house was extremely clean. The furniture was expensive but plain. She ushered me into the kitchen and put water on the stove for coffee. The stove, refrigerator, floor, and kitchen table were so clean, I felt uneasy. She carefully poured the hot water over the instant coffee and sat down across from me at the table. I couldn't get over the mechanical air about her. Almost as though she had been meeting Duke's women for a long time. How was I going to tell her that I was different? I was the one for Duke, and none of the other women he'd had were right for him.

Mrs. Ellsworth would have been very upset with my kitchen. I flashed on the dirty spaghetti dishes in the sink at home, on the unmade beds and unvacuumed rugs, on the decrepit couch. In our house, we took turns doing the housework, and everybody did as little as possible. I figured the kids' first priority was living. I knew mine was.

"I have these stupid old ladies I'm taking care of. They use the livingroom as a sitting room."

"Oh, that's okay. I like it here in the kitchen." I wanted to get right down to talking about Duke. "Don't you think it's awful that Duke's in that honor camp?"

"Yes, but I told him time after time, if he'd only turn to the Bible. I give him all the pamphlets that I get from my church, but he keeps right on drinking."

"Alcoholism is a disease, you know."

"He could stop if he wanted to. He just doesn't want to."

Someone called. A thin, high-pitched, weak screech.

"Excuse me a minute. That old fool is dying. She hasn't been out of bed in weeks. I told her son to come and take her out of here. I don't want her dying in my place, and she wants something every minute.

When she came back, I tried to talk about Duke again, but she continued to complain about the six old ladies she had boarding there.

"It's not easy. They shit in the bathtub and all over the bathroom floor, and I have to clean up after them. The Welfare pays for some of them, but no amount of money is enough for what I have to put up with. They got a real nice home here with me."

I thought, poor old ladies, to be trapped here.

I said, "Well, I guess I have to be going. It was nice visiting with you."

She walked me to the door.

"Nice to meet you. By the way, when you go the honor camp, let me know. I'll fix some fried chicken for Duke. You can stop by and pick it up."

When I go to the honor camp! How could I afford to drive sixty-five miles? One hundred and twelve, round trip? I didn't even have enough gas in the car to look for a job.

When I got home, I pulled the mail out of the box. I prayed there would be a child-support check. There wasn't. Karl had stopped paying again. I couldn't support us all on fifty-five dollars a week unemployment and I had missed a car payment. There was a notice from the Golden Door Finance Company about my overdue payment. Also a notice from the gas and electric company threatening to shut off my gas and lights if I didn't pay my bill, a couple of nasty notices from collection agencies for old, past due bills from my days of marriage to Karl, and a poor-me letter from Duke.

I wasn't home ten minutes when the phone rang.

"Is this Mrs. Hall?"

"No, this is Miss Hall."

"Oh. Well, I'm calling about your husband's loan on his 1961 Buick. The balance is five hundred dollars, and we can't seem to locate him."

"I don't know his present address. I'm not married to him any longer."

"Well, you signed the loan too, and we need the balance of the account or we're going to repossess the car."

"I don't have the car. It was awarded to him. I won't make payments on his car."

"Mrs. Hall, if we can't find him, you are responsible legally for the balance of this account."

"Good. Put me in jail. I could use a rest right about now."

"Is there any way you could make a partial payment?"

"No! I'm unemployed and trying to raise six kids. He doesn't send us our child-support money either. He owes me a lot more than he owes you."

"If we could just have your word that you would send us a small payment, we could keep this out of court."

"He works for I.T.&T., you know. That's International Telephone and Telegraph Company—the biggest fucking company in the world. Ask them!"

I slammed the phone down. It rang again and I didn't answer. They finally gave up.

There wasn't much to eat in the house, so I walked to Harry's Market and bought a package of hot dogs, a loaf of bread, and a half gallon of milk. I cut the hot dogs in two so it would look like more and put the super-sized peanut butter jar in the middle of the table. I had about three dollars left.

I sat on the couch and noticed that more and more springs were working their way through. I tried to think of something that would help our dilemma and nothing came to me.

I called a woman friend, and she suggested I go to the District Attorney's office and file a complaint against Karl to get the child-support money. That sounded reasonable because I couldn't ask my lawyer friend to do anything more. I owed him hundreds of dollars and he had never sent a bill.

The next morning, after the children ate their corn flakes and went to school, I put a dollar's worth of gas in the car and drove downtown to the courthouse. I took the elevator to the seventh floor and walked into a waiting room.

There were several women with children, waiting to be interviewed. They were shabby and haggard. Abandoned mothers have premature lines on their faces, mouths that never smile. One was screaming at her little boy.

"Get the hell over here and sit down, or I'll smash you up against the wall."

I walked up to the counter and told the woman my name.

"Have you ever filled out an absent-father form?"

"Well, you'll have to take this form home, fill it out and mail it back in," she said, mechanically shoving the paper at me.

"Can't I fill it out here and leave it?"

"I'm sorry, but those are the rules. You fill out the form, and we'll give you an appointment, probably in about a month."

"A month! But I have to see someone today! I don't have any money."

I felt like crying.

"I'm sorry. Please step aside."

I took the form and caught the elevator back down to the ground floor. When I got home, I told the children what had happened. They could see how beat I was and told me they would get jobs. Tim had already applied for a dishwashing job at a pancake house.

I went to bed and prayed. "Mother God, just give me a chance. I'll do anything. I'll help us if you'll just show me how." I waited for an answer, an idea. None came. What more could I do? I was putting first things first, living one day at a time, and praying for guidance to keep the family afloat. I would do anything, anything I could.

I felt as though I were hanging on the edge of a cliff by my fingernails, and the raging sea was waiting below.

The next day a fifty-dollar check from Karl arrived in the mail. It wasn't much, but it was fifty dollars more than I had. I thought of putting an ad in the paper and letting people know I was looking for a job. It might get results and was worth a try.

I drove downtown to the newspaper office. "I would like to place an ad in the paper for a job," I told the man behind the counter.

"Okay. How would you like it to read?"

"Draftswoman, excellent ink work, needs work."

"Draftswoman?" He looked puzzled.

"Yes. I'm a woman, and I want employers to know that."

"But there's no such word as draftswoman."

"Well, there is now," I snapped.

"I don't know if that's acceptable. Wait here a minute."

He called another man over. They whispered a minute, and then the second man spoke. "I don't think we can print that word because there is no such word."

I was getting angry. "I'm a woman and not a *draftsman*. And it's my ad."

"I'll have to call the editor to see if it's all right to use it."

"You must be kidding me. You mean you have to check with the editor just because I want to use the word 'drafts-woman'? What's the big deal?"

The men were nervous about my growing anger. One stepped back to the phone and called the editor, talking with his back to me so I couldn't hear.

They finally told me the editor had given his permission for me to put the word "draftswoman" in my ad. What a small right to have to fight for. Seeds were being planted in my head, one by one.

I got home and found that David had washed some-one's car, Susan was baby-sitting for the woman next door, and Tim would be working at the pancake house after school and on Saturdays. They handed me six dollars and forty cents. I cried.

Susan had been telling me for a long time that she wanted to get out of the special class, and I promised her I would call the teacher. The three boys were doing fairly well in school. Their report cards weren't the best in the world, but they were passing.

I talked to Susan's teacher. "Susan tells me she wants to get out of your class and into regular classes. She thinks she's ready."

"Oh, I don't know about that. She's doing very well here."

"She says she'll never know how well she can do in a regular class if she doesn't at least try."

"I know, but if she failed, she would be far worse off psychologically than she is now. Maybe we can talk about it at the end of the semester."

"All right. I'll explain it to her."

I called Susan. "I just talked to your teacher."

Her eyes lit up. "Oh, what did she say? Can I go into a regular class?"

"Mrs. Houseman feels you should stay until the end of the year, and then we can decide what to do."

Susan screamed, "Mom, that class is filled with abnormal kids and kids from bad families. All we ever learn is two plus two is four and four plus four is eight! All I do all day long is fix the bulletin board, take care of the chalk boards and help her with the bad kids. I'm sick of it!"

"Okay, honey." I wanted to help get her out, but I didn't know how to get around the system. "Can't you just make it through the end of the year? Then we'll do something for sure."

She saw I was helpless. "Okay, Mom. I'll try, but I really want to be in regular classes next year."

A few days later I got a job.

I got a call from a civil engineer in answer to my ad. I went for the interview and got the job. My starting salary was two fifty an hour, which was fifty cents more than I had made at the shipbuilding company. I had to learn to draw subdivision maps in ink.

I didn't care what I had to do, I was so glad to be working again. Finally I would get back into the swing of regular paychecks and helping my family to survive.

I had filled out the papers from the DA's office, answering all the personal questions which made me feel I was the criminal instead of Karl. I mailed in the form and got a letter back, telling me the date of my interview. My interviewer was a man. I wondered if he would be on my side.

Duke was writing every day, begging me to drive up to the honor camp. I tried to tell him in my letters that I had to take care of my family, and he always answered with a lot of fatherly advice which I guess he thought would help the children through osmosis.

In the meantime, Chris called me from somewhere and said he was coming home to visit for a couple of days. I couldn't go see Duke because I was looking forward to seeing Chris and having a long talk with him. He arrived home on Wednesday, and when I got home from work, there he was—in an Air Force uniform.

We hugged. "Chris, what's this all about?"

"Well, Mom, I was going to get drafted anyway, so I decided to join the Air Force and get the damned thing over with."

"Mother God," I gasped. "What if they sent you to Vietnam?"

The whole thing exploded in my brain. The Vietnam fighting was just getting underway, and I hadn't even had time to think much about it. Now here I was, standing in my livingroom with my arms around a man in uniform, this time my son. It made me sick.

"Hopefully not," Chris said. "I have a better chance in the Air Force of staying out of it."

I just couldn't assimilate the facts. It seemed so wrong. Chris, now twenty, had been away from home for three years, working at numerous jobs in Santa Cruz. He had been a dishwasher at Woolworths, then a bellhop, a gas station attendant, a waiter, and finally a desk clerk at one of the hotels. He had been going to college at the same time, and I had sent him fifteen or twenty dollars when I could, which wasn't often. He was a beautiful, motivated young man, and now, at the peak of his young life, he was an Airman Third Class with a chance at being sent to somebody else's war, to be maimed or killed.

I felt guilty too. Guilty for not helping him financially, guilty for not being a better mother, a perfect mother. And guilty for not having told him the truth—that Karl was not his father.

When everyone was fed and watching TV, I asked Chris to go out to the porch with me.

44

I was scared and could hardly start talking as we sat on the steps.

"Chris, I have something to tell you that I should have told you a long time ago. I guess things come in their right time. I don't know if this is the right time or not, but I have to take a chance."

"What is it, Mom?"

"How do you feel about Karl? As a father, I mean."

He shrugged. "I'll probably never see him again. Why?"

"Well, during the war, World War II, things were all mixed up. People were mixed up too. Living was really intense. We were all saying, 'Eat, drink, and be merry for tomorrow we may all die.' We were young and that's exactly what we did. Can you understand that?"

"Sure."

"Well, we all did things we wouldn't ordinarily do. I met an Air Force pilot and fell in love. He got shot down and killed in the war. And I was pregnant. With you. He was your father, Chris, not Karl."

Chris wasn't looking at me. I sat beside him shaking. I heard the telephone ring in the distance and wondered if I was doing the right thing. Was I just getting it off my conscience? But he had a right to know.

Colleen called me from the door. "It's Duke, Mom. Long distance."

My brain whirled in confusion. I was furious with Duke, calling at that moment. He was getting more and more demanding.

"Go on and answer it," Chris told me in a quiet voice.

Duke's voice over the phone said, "Nancy, I got a chance to get to a phone. When are you coming to see me? Can you make it on Sunday?"

"Okay, Duke, I'll try to get there next Sunday."

"What's wrong with your voice? Is everything okay?"

I had just dropped a bomb on my oldest son, who was out on the porch waiting for an explanation, and my lover was calling me from prison.

"I have a little problem right now."

"With what?"

"With one of the children. It's all right, Duke."

I couldn't cut him off and yet I had cut off my own son. The guilt was eating me up.

"Do you love me, Nancy?"

"Yes, Duke, I love you and I'll be there Sunday."

"Okay, I gotta go now. They're waiting to take me back."

I hung up and ran back out to the porch.

Chris looked at me, still stunned. "I can't believe what you've told me."

"I know." I didn't know. I could see how white he was.

"What was he like?"

"He was a wonderful man, Chris. A lot like you. And I can tell you, he really loved me. He was serious and gentle, smart in a deep way. I didn't drink when I was going with him. That's how good he was."

"Why didn't you get married?"

"He wanted to wait until after the war. He was a Flying Tiger pilot."

"Why did you marry Karl?"

"I wanted you to have a father. I didn't know where to turn after Joe died, was killed."

"Was that his name? Joe?"

"Yes. Joe." He was going to ask me Joe's last name and I was going to have to tell him I didn't know. I had never known, or I had heard it and forgotten. It hadn't seemed important, but I know it was to Chris. "I've forgotten his last name, Chris." Tears sprung to my eyes as I faced him. "I hope you don't hate me."

"I don't hate you, Mom. It's just a shock, that's all."

I hugged him. He was crying, and we wept in each other's arms.

Chris left on Friday. When we said goodbye, he hugged me and said, "It's hard, Mom, but don't worry. I'll be okay."

"I know you will, Chris. You're a fine young man. I hope you never have to go to Vietnam, though. I couldn't stand that."

"I couldn't handle it either, Mom."

Sunday I filled my work thermos with coffee, bought a carton of cigarettes for Duke, which I couldn't afford, and picked up Mrs. Ellsworth's fried chicken. I left at eight-thirty, not wanting to be a minute late for visiting hours at the honor camp. They started at eleven.

It was a beautiful, sunny morning, and as I drove up into the mountains, I became more and more excited about seeing Duke. The other part of me was fearful and guilt-ridden.

Mary was keeping an eye on the children, but I had never gone so far away from them. What if I had car trouble and couldn't get back? The closer I got to the honor camp, the further away my thoughts got from the children.

I arrived too early and parked by a big tree, waiting for time to pass. Finally I saw by the car clock that it was eleven. I drove through the prison gate, and a correctional officer motioned me on to the visitors' parking lot. Then he came up to my car and asked me who I was visiting.

By the time I locked the car and started walking toward the gate, I saw Duke coming down a hill, obviously from the barracks-type buildings I saw on the hill. It reminded me of an Army camp in old war movies. The difference was it was in the majestic mountains where everything smelled and looked fresh and alive.

Wow, I thought, this isn't such a bad place to be. I wouldn't mind a vacation at a camp like this.

Duke was smiling. We hugged and kissed, and he said, "Come on, let's go over there to the picnic tables and sit."

I opened the thermos and poured some coffee into the top. He opened the chicken.

"Boy, this is good. Did you make it, doll?"

"No, your mother did."

Immediately, his face changed. He stiffened. "Oh, I guess you met my mother then."

"Yes, she seems really nice."

"Yep, she's had a hard life. After my dad died, she didn't have any income, so she started renting her rooms to old ladies. She's doing okay now. But I don't want to talk about her."

His expression changed back to one of joy and laughter. "You're lookin' good, baby."

"You look good too, Duke."

We kissed again.

"Let's eat some chicken before I screw you right here," he said. We ate and talked about the camp, the kids, my new job, and how tough it would be waiting the three months for him to get out.

"Listen, babe, I know if you can find me a good attorney that a judge would let me out early. Will you do that?"

"I don't know any attorneys, Duke."

"There's one in AA. I think his name is Bardin. Would you call him and ask him to come up and see me?"

I was not going to call the attorney in AA. What did Duke think AA was for anyway? Free legal counsel?

We had straddled the bench, facing each other. Now we moved closer and closer, touching each other and kissing. Duke rubbed my breasts, took my hand and put it on his hard penis. "Feel that, baby?"

"I can't take this, Duke! I'm moving to the other side of the table."

"Shit, babe, that's how couples screw in here. Right on these benches, facing each other. Come on, sweetie, let's try it."

"Duke, I can't. The guards are looking."

"Hell, they know what's going on. They turn their backs. Haven't I made you hot, doll? I'm hot as a firecracker!"

"I won't do it here, Duke." I got up and moved across the table from him. I hadn't come expecting sex or privacy, but Duke had turned me on, and I was frustrated and upset. I figured he was as disappointed as I was, however, and didn't want to take my feelings out on him.

"Okay, okay," he said. "Well, I got another idea anyway. I'll fix it up for us next time."

I nodded and looked around at the other women who had come up to visit the prisoners. Mothers, girlfriends, sisters, wives, and even grandmothers. Most were talking loudly to the men they were sitting with, motioning with their hands, pointing their fingers. There wasn't a happy face in the whole group.

I suddenly saw myself as one of these women and asked myself, what are we all doing here? The dark thought lasted only a second, and then I was back listening to Duke, who was into a tirade about the injustice of putting drunks in jail.

"What are these other men in for?" I asked.

"Some for drunk. Others for non-support. Those are the bastards I hate. Like Karl. Those sons-of-bitches should be hung by the balls. There ain't no justice when drunks are stuck in with pricks who don't support their kids. I tell you, I got no use for men who don't support their families."

"They'll never catch up with Karl."

"You just keep after the DA. They can get him in another state if they want to."

When visiting hours were over, Duke walked me back to my car. He squeezed me so hard I thought my ribs would break.

"I love you, Duke," I said between kisses.

"Me too, doll."

We were getting ourselves worked up again. He pulled me around behind the car and got his hands under my blouse.

"Don't worry, baby. I'll figure something out."

I was frustrated. My head was pounding.

"Duke, I have to go now."

"Okay, doll. Write me every day now. I just go berserk when I don't get a letter."

I drove away quickly. When I got to the highway, I pulled over and masturbated myself to orgasm. Love, sexual desire, passion, compulsion, addiction, needing and wanting.

The closer I got to home, the more certain I was that something had happened to the children. Nothing had happened. Mary had everything under control and was getting ready to go out for the evening.

"How late are you going to be out?" I asked.

"Oh, I don't know. I'll probably be home early."

"Can I ask you something?"

"Sure."

"Are you drinking? I thought I smelled alcohol on you the other night."

"Mother, everyone who drinks isn't an alcoholic!"

"I know that. I'm not stupid. I just asked you."

"I'm a big girl now. Will you leave me alone?"

"I do leave you alone, but I can't stand you staying out all night much longer. You're either going to have to get a job or go to school."

"Okay, okay! How about if I move out?"

"Where to? You don't even have a job."

"I'll find a place. And I'll get a job tomorrow."

"Fine with me, then. Move out."

I didn't know how to handle Mary. We had been fighting more and more. No matter what I said, she insisted that she was grown up and able to take care of herself. My futile attempts to be both mother and father were chipping away at both of us. I was beginning to realize I couldn't be both, but assumed that was because I wasn't wise enough. All the years I had been drunk, Mary had been mother to her brothers and sisters, and she was very independent. I felt I owed her all the freedom I could give her, but when she stayed out until four in the morning, I couldn't sleep because of the endless horrors my imagination invented.

The following day, Mary got a job at the pancake house where Tim worked and, with the small amount of money she had saved, moved into a tiny apartment on an alley in Mission Beach.

Her first night away from home, she phoned.

"Can I come home and sleep on the couch? There's someone screaming in the alley."

"Stay inside until you see my car. I'll be right over."

I drove down the boulevard and into the alley in record time. When Mary got into the car, she showed me the kitchen knife she had in her pocket.

"It was eerie, Mom. I was scared."

"Me too."

"My first night out on my own, and I'm going back home to sleep on the couch," she complained.

I hugged her. "I'm glad," I said.

After that, Mary stayed in her apartment and managed her own life. I later found out that she had a man staying with her. She had known him in school. They had fallen in love and wanted to get married. I talked to her about it, and she convinced me it was the right thing to do. I agreed because I didn't know anything else was possible for a young woman. At least she will be taken care of, I thought, and I won't have to worry about her anymore.

51

Seth was an artist, specializing in cartooning, posters, murals for businesses, and psychedelic artwork. I liked him. He showed me some of the cartoon strips he had drawn when he was very young. They had been published in one of the local papers. I was impressed. What I didn't know was that Seth had been smoking marijuana since he was fourteen and had embarked on several trips with LSD.

Mary and Seth wanted a "mod" wedding, so I took my two hundred dollars out of savings and bought Mary a short white lace dress that she wore with silver stockings.

Thus, my oldest daughter became a bride.

I had to take time off work to keep my appointment with the District Attorney's office. The male interviewer told me it was almost impossible to catch up with Karl. He wanted to know everything about me: my bills, my salary, the children's ages, and personal information that I felt had nothing to do with whether Karl should pay child-support or not. Finally the man told me that if Florida, where Karl was living, was one of the states California had reciprocal agreements with, they might cooperate. At any rate, he said, it would take time.

I was feeling bitter as I left the office. It was almost impossible, in other words, to get fathers to pay child support if they didn't want to. It didn't matter that Karl had a good job with I.T.&T. I began to suspect that the important job protected him. If the law hounded anybody, it was probably the jobless and minority fathers. I also knew that if Karl or any father were caught, he could hand the judge ten dollars, and in the court's eyes, that would be an attempt to pay.

On Mission Beach things were happening.

The face of Mission Boulevard was changing. Psychedelic shops were appearing everywhere, buildings painted with weird designs. Color was everywhere, especially in the thrift-store clothes of the long-haired young adults. The music was hard rock music: the Beatles, the Rolling Stones, the Kinks, the Doors, Love, the Animals, Blue Cheer, Jefferson Airplane, and the Dave Clark Five. All that music blasted out from the beach house behind the trolley station and from the shacks all up and down Mission Boulevard.

I thought it was dramatic. I had always loved drama. I also loved change, and things were definitely changing. There was something more important festering underneath it all. People had been getting more and more upset about the Vietnam War. Young men let their hair grow long and sat on the sidewalks on Mission Boulevard with signs that read "Peace and Love" and "Make Love Not War." Television was showing us disruptions at the universities. I sympathized with their drop-out philosophy.

The people I agreed with were speaking up. I had lived through World War II and the Korean War, and I was cynical. If the politicians and generals knew that they would have to fight on the front lines of any war, perhaps they would begin to look for peaceful solutions.

Tim, Steve, and David spent most of their time out back in the beach shack. Their psychedelic posters, fish nets, and surf boards filled the place. Tim played the guitar, and that brought many friends in to visit. They were smoking pot, but as long as they didn't bring it into the house, I was comfortable. I didn't like it, but I knew from my own experience of using alcohol and pills that I couldn't stop the boys from experimenting.

"What you do outside the house is your business, but until you pay the rent, I don't want drugs or alcohol in the house where I live," I said. They respected my wishes, probably because they had lived through such horror with me when I was a user.

Many of the young people that hung around the beach shack came into the house to visit me. My door was always open. I knew some of them were stoned, but how could I sit in judgment? I prayed that I would serve as a good example.

I knew I was fortunate to have a little more information about addiction than a lot of other parents. Nothing short of chaining them to the bedpost could stop young people from doing whatever it was they wanted. In my own case, Karl couldn't beat me into stopping drinking. The law couldn't force me, the shrinks couldn't brainwash me, and the ministers could neither inspire me or shame me into stopping. I stopped when I came to the end, when I was almost dead.

It was ironic that I knew this about my children but continued to be obsessed with the idea that I could change Duke.

I came home from work one day and was talking to a friend on the phone. I loved talking on the phone to friends. It was like a microphone. I was on stage, and the person on the other end had to listen.

The kids were running in and out and making a lot of noise.

"Would you please shut up and let me talk on the phone," I yelled.

Colleen ran into the room. "Come into the other room," she told Susan. "I've got to tell you something."

I didn't pay much attention. I was still talking when Susan came to stand over me.

"I have something important to tell you, Mom. It's an emergency."

"Okay, what is it?" I asked, my hand over the phone.

"Colleen just told me there was a man leaning up against the telephone pole in the alley."

"And?"

"And he was doing something."

"Well, he just had on bathing shorts, and he had his thing out when Colleen and Patty walked by."

I said goodbye quickly and hung up the phone. "Where's Colleen now, Susan?"

"She's gone outside with Patty."

"Show me where the man is."

"Oh, he left, and they went to Patty's house."

"Are you sure he's gone?"

"Yeah. Colleen didn't want me to tell you because she didn't want to stay in the house."

"Go get her. I'm calling the police right now."

The police came and questioned Colleen and Patty. The little girls said the man was old but not too old, medium tall, and had on bathing trunks.

"What are you going to do?" I asked the police.

"We'll keep an eye out for him in the neighborhood, but I suggest you keep your little girl close to home. You never know how dangerous these people are."

The next day two plain clothes detectives went to Colleen's school to question the children. The principal called me at work and said the man fit the description of a child molester they had been looking for on the other side of town. He suggested I keep Colleen close to home until they picked up the man.

Keep Colleen closer to home?

My children had roamed the beach for almost two years. They knew all the neighbors, the storekeepers, the hippies, the surfers, and everyone else living in this gigantic beach family where everyone took care of everyone else. The children's freedom was not being threatened by young men with long hair, by drug users, by bikers, or by psychedelic lovers. It was being threatened by a fifty-year-old, job-holding, short-haired jerk.

While the pervert was at large, I kept a butcher knife under the bed. If only Duke would get out of the honor camp right now and come home to protect us.

I sat in front of the television, watching the news. The college students were fighting against the stupidity of the war, and the Pentagon's war machine was in high gear.

I had so many problems I felt as though I were trying to keep a sand castle together while the tide came in. Chris was already in the Air Force, and Tim was getting older. Duke was scheduled to get out of the honor camp. Susan wanted to get out of the special class. David's school called and said he was suspended for setting off the fire alarm and putting cherry bombs in the toilets. Steve was piling up old bicycle parts by the house. Tim wanted to buy a GTO with his minimum-wage salary from the pancake house. My job was almost over because the company had no new contract. I had had no child-support money or word from the District Attorney's office. The trolley station had been sold, and the new landlord couldn't make up his mind if he wanted us to stay as tenants or not. Then Mary phoned.

"Hi, Mom. I'm pregnant."

Duke called from the Sheriff's Release Station in San Diego. He was out of the honor camp and wanted me to pick him up. I felt ten million butterflies in my stomach and couldn't get there fast enough.

When I arrived, he was sitting in the lobby with a brown paper bag on his lap: his worldly possessions. As I walked toward him, he smiled, and we grabbed each other as though we were a couple of leeches. He looked very healthy and happy, and I felt sure he had learned his lesson. I thought anyone could stay sober because I was sober.

We got into my car to drive home and I asked where he wanted to go.

"To bed with you—what else?"

"I'm so glad to see you, Duke. I missed you so much."

Duke put his hand on my crotch. "I missed you too, doll, and I missed this most of all."

"Duke, I'm trying to drive."

He stretched out and slid down in the seat. "Boy, freedom! I ain't never going to go to jail again. Those bastards are never going to get me again."

I smiled happily behind the wheel and thought, he's never going to drink again.

The magnificent obsession—mine, his or anybody's—to live in illusions. To force life to go our way and never to accept it as it is. I had been that way drunk, and now I was that way sober.

I parked the car behind the trolley station, and we got out. Duke noticed my new bumper sticker, "Make Love Not War," as we passed.

"What the hell is that all about?"

"What's the matter with it?"

"Don't you know we have to be in Vietnam to fight? Do you want the Commies to come in and take us over?"

"Do you want Tim to go to war?"

"I had to go to war. I wanted to fight for my country. We have to protect our country. But, hell, I wouldn't expect you to understand. Women think differently."

"You mean I can't think or have a valid opinion?"

He patted me on the ass as we walked to the house. "It's okay, honey, you just let us men take care of the important things."

"How the hell many wars do we have to fight before we kill all the young men?" I argued. "If the big shots who start the wars never have to do the fighting and dying, when will it stop?"

"Wars are necessary, you know that."

"No, I don't know it!"

"Don't you want to protect your freedom and all the things this country has fought so hard for?"

"I don't think we're fighting for freedom. I think we're fighting for power, so the rich old men can get richer. My bumper sticker stays on."

Duke was furious. "You are a crazy bitch."

He forgot about the fight as soon as we got inside and said hello to the children. As soon as the kids went about their business, Duke pulled me into the bedroom, closed the door, and took off his clothes. I didn't feel much like making love. I was still upset about the fight, but I had been horny for so long, I forced myself to go along. It didn't work.

Duke propped himself against the headboard and lit a cigarette. "Did you like that, babe?"

"Sure, Duke," I lied.

"Am I better than Karl was?"

I laughed. "What do you want to know that for?"

"Oh, come on, doll. You can tell me. Did he have a big cock?"

"What difference does it make?"

"Oh! It makes a lot of difference. Women like big cocks."

"Duke, I don't want to talk about it."

"Just answer the question. Did he have a bigger cock than me?"

"Yes, yes, yes. He had a bigger prick than you, but he beat me every day, so what the hell difference does it make whether or not he was big? I hated him."

He pulled me toward him and kissed me. Then he went to sleep. I got up and started supper.

The new owners of the trolley station came by and told me that I could continue to rent the house. That was one worry out of the way.

It looked as though Duke had moved in to stay, and I wasn't sure I wanted that. He was causing me more trouble than another child. On the other hand, if he had left, I would have been heart-broken.

Chris didn't have to go to Vietnam. They sent him to India instead.

He had married a young woman he met in Santa Cruz: Lori. I received a letter from him asking me if Lori could come and live with us while he was overseas. I said yes.

I was happy to see Lori when she arrived. I remembered the early years with Karl and how I suffered when he went overseas. At least Chris didn't want to be a career man. He would leave the Air Force as soon as his time was up. I hoped the noise and confusion of our family life would help Lori. She did her best to be cheerful, but I sensed her loneliness for Chris.

I didn't know how to explain Duke to her. He wasn't working but he was making an effort to find a job. My job was shaky, and I felt comfort having another woman in the house, thinking she could help me solve some problems. She tried, but she couldn't possibly help me with my problems. Nobody could.

The greatest relief was that she was going to be at the house while I was at work. She cleaned every day and kept track of the children. It was a big job.

Duke found a job at the shipyards and asked me to marry him. He wanted to drive to Yuma and get married on Christmas Eve. Lori was excited and said she'd take care of things at the house. I was reluctant to leave the children on Christmas Eve, but when Duke spent his entire paycheck for a pile of presents for the kids—forgetting about the rent—I agreed, provided we were home for Christmas.

59

Lori bought me a pretty blue shorty nightgown with ruffles all over it for the honeymoon. I packed a small suitcase, and we left in my car, with Duke driving. I had my paycheck for the gas money, motel, food, and marriage expenses. I felt safe with Lori at home and in charge.

As we drove the hundred and sixty-nine miles to Yuma, I floated in whimsical fantasy. Duke was the perfect man for me, tall and handsome and sober forevermore. He loved the children and he was working. Family responsibility would be good for him, keep him involved and away from temptation. The thrill of getting married, the act itself, filled me with love and optimism. It was going to be really beautiful, our life together, and everything would be all right forever after.

The desert at dusk was a flat, barren wilderness. A few cacti reached toward the pink and black sky like birthday candles on a huge cake. I sat snuggled close to Duke, feeling the heat of his body, his hand warm on my leg, and watched the moon appear to light up the whole desert. It was full and bigger than I'd ever seen it. I felt it envelop me, embracing me and the entire earth.

Suddenly, Duke pulled off the highway onto a side trail.

"What are you doing, honey?" I looked at him and knew.

He stopped the car and put the seat down in a horizontal position. He opened the back of the wagon so we could see out, and we fucked. I felt cheated. He didn't give me a chance to have an orgasm. The romantic promise of the setting had collaped.

Duke was in high spirits. He drove on to Yuma. We got a blood test at a raunchy doctor's office, went to a commercial chapel, and got married by a justice of the peace. I paid him ten dollars. I was a bride again: December 24, 1966.

When we walked into the office to register for the motel, Duke spotted a rack of books about Yuma, Arizona. After he had paid for the room with money I'd given him, he bought a book from the rack: *The Hell Hole*. It was about the territorial prison in Yuma. He loved books about prisons.

In our room, I immediately took a shower and put on the frilly nightie. I walked into the bedroom expecting to make the wedding bells sing out. Duke was propped up in bed reading his book.

"Oh, hi, doll. Boy, this little book is really good stuff."

I got into bed and curled up beside him. "Duke, this is our honeymoon."

He kissed me on the cheek and went back to reading. I finally fell asleep.

In the morning, he laughed. "Well, I fucked you in the desert, didn't I? What about that?"

"That was fine," I lied again.

"Look, honey. I'd like to go visit this prison it talks about in the book. We can do it before we start back to San Diego."

"If that's what you want to do, sure."

I didn't really know what was missing, but I wasn't going to let my disappointment spoil my fantasy of love. I could change him, make him into a perfect husband. With so much love between us, I could do anything.

We visited the Territorial Prison, which was depressing. It would never be on my list of favorite tourist attractions of the West. As we walked through the grim fortress and peered into the cells with their dirt floors, I shuddered at the whole concept of locking people up. The book told of two women in the prison: Pearl Hart, in for armed robbery since 1899, and Isabella Washington, imprisoned at age nineteen for manslaughter.

Back in San Diego, the children were glad to see us and showed us all their Christmas presents. Lori, smiling, said everything had been fine.

We began our new married life, Duke and I, with both of us working. I believed the two paychecks would cover all the bills and allow us to live in comfort. Duke worked overtime on Saturdays, which gave us even more money. The first week was blissful.

On Saturday of the second week, Duke came home at ten o'clock in the morning with a 1959 Chevy.

"Well, I finally found a car for myself," he announced.

"How much?" I asked, going to him for a kiss.

"I gave the guy three hundred for it. It was my paycheck, but after all, honey, I do need a car."

I smelled something familiar.

"Do you think we can afford it right now?"

He reached over to grab me. "It's all right, baby. You're my sweet little thing, aren't you?"

I knew.

"You've been drinking, Duke," I cried. "How could you do that?"

I knew how he could do it. I had done it for twenty years. It was easy, a lot easier than staying sober and facing reality, easier than watching other people turn in on themselves with drugs and alcohol and remaining an observer.

"What are you talking about? I'm okay. It's just your imagination," Duke protested.

"I know booze when I smell it."

"I gotta go now. The guy's waiting for me to decide."

"You better not drive when you're drinking."

"I'm okay, damn it! I'll see you later."

I was scared. Being an alcoholic, I knew one drink led to another. Next time I saw Duke, would he be drunk? Mother God, why had I married him? Why had I chained myself to a drunk?

I couldn't write that night. I couldn't do anything except wait, dreading the inevitable. Finally I phoned his mother on the chance he had gone over to her house. She promptly told me that if he was drunk, there was no telling what he would do.

"He just can't stay away from that booze," she said. "I've told him a million times that he had to turn to God or he'll go straight to hell and burn in the fire."

I wondered if he had listened to that all his life.

I hung up the phone and felt more fearful than ever. When the children asked about Duke, I had to tell them. I was embarassed for Lori to hear about it. I had wanted to make a good impression on her, and now I had blown it. She tried to reassure me. What did she know about alcoholism?

Duke didn't come home that night or the next day.

Sunday night, he staggered in drunk and roaring. The children were outside playing, but Lori was there with me.

"Who the hell's been here? What man are you screwing? Show me the son-of-a-bitch, and I'll kill the bastard."

Lori's eyes popped, but I was terrified. It was pure nonsense, but he meant it.

"There's no one here, Duke," I said, motioning Lori back into the kitchen. "What are you talking about?"

"You know what I'm talking about! That punk kid that lives behind us. That fucker who says he's an artist. He's fucking you, and don't try to tell me different."

Weaving back and forth, he started toward me.

"Call the police, Lori! Hurry!"

"Go ahead, call the police. This is my house, and I'm not having any punk kid screwing you, you bitch." While he yelled, he swept Tim's guitar up off the couch and smashed it across the coffee table. Then he half fell, half sat down in the old rocker.

I waited, filled with fury and fear. The fear kept me quiet.

The police arrived almost immediately. Duke was sitting meekly in the rocker, but the guitar lay demolished on the floor.

"Get him out of my house," I told the officer.

"Is he your husband?"

"Yes."

"Well, I can't take him out of his own home."

"What? Can't you see he's violent? Look at what he did to my son's guitar!"

Duke had a drunken smirk on his face. I wanted to kill him.

"Sorry, lady. The only way we can take him in is if you make a citizen's arrest."

"Okay, how do I do that? I refuse to have him in the house with my kids. He's crazy drunk."

"Just say you arrest him."

Duke mumbled in a pitiful voice. "Oh, honey, you don't want to do that."

"Oh yes I do. I arrest you, right now!"

Duke got up, staggering. "I'm okay, officer. I'm okay."

"Sorry, buddy, but I have to take you in."

The two officers took Duke by the arms, and Duke blubbered all the way out. I turned to Lori with tears in my eyes.

"I'm sorry you had to witness such a thing."

"Maybe he'll be all right after this."

I broke down crying. "Oh, Lori, I don't know. I should never have married him. I thought he'd stay sober. He's a totally different person when he's drunk." I saw the smashed guitar through my tears and wailed. "What am I going to tell Tim?"

Tim was furious. "Who did that?" he yelled.

"Duke. He was drunk and violent. We called the police. It would have been one of us next." I was crushed with guilt, seeing the grief on his face. "I'll buy you a new one, Tim, as soon as I get the money."

"That guitar's my whole life, Mom. I want to be a musician. I'm not going to work in a restaurant the rest of my life! Shit!"

"I'm so sorry, Tim. Please don't yell at me."

"Why don't you get rid of that guy? He's nothing but a drunk! You deserve better than that!"

Tim collapsed on the couch. His long curly hair fell over his face, and the tears flowed. He had been working very hard to get a car with his money, and the loss of the guitar was a real blow. I had no idea when I could get together enough money to replace it.

I sat on the couch beside him, and he put his arms around me.

"I know you need love, too, Mom. It's okay." I knew then that my sixteen-year-old son was already more grown up than Duke.

After the guitar incident, I lost my fairy-tale illusions.

I faced the fact that Duke was always going to be trouble. I had been trying to mold him into something I thought he should be. I finally accepted the clay crumbling in my hands and let it fall.

I thought about the fact that both the police and Duke had called the trolley station his home. No way was this Duke's house. I had always paid the rent, every penny. The furniture was all mine. The house belonged to my family, and Duke had nothing to do with it. He was only a house guest, and that only if he stayed sober.

Duke got out of jail and got drunk again. When they sent him back to the honor camp for three more months, I called my lawyer to get a divorce.

It was a simple divorce because Duke had such a long record. The day I went to court, everything moved very fast. I sat in the witness stand, and after my lawyer spoke, the old judge leaned over to me, pushed his glasses down on his nose, and peered over the tops.

"I bet you thought you could save him."

"You're right. I did."

"Divorce granted."

I left the court feeling free. Now I was responsible only for the children and myself again. No man would ever try to rule my Queendom again, I vowed. I would stay independent. Any man in my life, from now on, including Duke, would stay in his proper role: playmate, not lifemate.

At the same time, I wasn't at all sure a woman with five children could survive with dignity without a man.

Working in engineering at a drawing board all day had its liabilities.

I learned early to do my work well and not be bothered by a supervisor hanging over my shoulder. I made myself ignore what I was drawing—whether building plans that gouged the earth or government contracts that gouged the taxpayers.

My easiest jobs were defense contracts. With these, the management was usually lax and the draftspeople were not pushed. It made me mad that the war protesters going to Canada were called traitors and these businessmen were considered good citizens. There was a common saying around the offices then: "It's good enough for government work." Later, the saying became "It's good enough for nuke work."

66

Civil engineering was almost as frustrating for me as helping to install missiles on warships. The builders were tearing up the earth as thoughtlessly as children. No analyzing of space, no innovative ideas for using the natural curves of the earth. Just level the hills to flatland for easier, quicker profits. Get those steam shovels and iron toys moving.

I liked to draw, however, and found satisfaction in completing a good drawing. I was usually the only woman in the drafting room and I learned to fit in by being quiet and not relating to the men sexually. But once they got to know me, they felt free to try and include me in their rotten jokes about women, saying, "Oh, you're just one of the guys now, Nancy."

Even at that, they had some sort of sixth sense about me and never dared touch my body. I walked away from the dirty jokes but the story would have been different had they tried to pinch me or touch me. I have never been afraid to make a scene!

And they did respect my work. Why not? I was working twice as hard as the men because I was a woman and had to prove myself worthy in their world.

Whenever the work load slowed down and there were no new contracts, half of us would be laid off, and I would be back in the unemployment line. I often stood as long as three hours in that line, and saw people collapse on the floor or throw up. The ambulance was a regular visitor at the unemployment office. I was getting used to being treated like a sub-human.

The sixty-two dollars a week I got on unemployment was never enough to keep my family going, so I would refinance my car with the Golden Door Finance Company and "start over." Always, when I was looking for a job, any job would do. I would answer every ad in the paper for a drafter and finally I would get a job. My pay now was $3.50 an hour, the most I had made so far. It was very important for me to work: more than money, I earned dignity.

I received a letter from Duke at the honor camp.

He said he didn't blame me for getting the divorce and apologized for his behavior. "Nancy, you need someone better than me," he wrote. "I love you more than anything in the world, but you need a stable person. I'm no good for you."

I should have stopped reading right there. Curiosity made me continue.

"I really miss you and I pray that you will at least come and see me. We had some good fuckin', didn't we? If you could find it in your heart to forgive me, I will never drink again. Some of the guys have been escaping and meeting their broads by the rest stop on the highway. We could do that and go screw someplace, and then I could walk back to the camp. Write me a letter right away and tell me if you want to meet me this Sunday at nine in the morning. I sure will be praying that you will. I want to feel your body next to mine again. Love ya, doll. Duke."

He did it again. He turned me on. I was so lonely and horny that I sat right down and wrote him back saying I would be there at nine.

I got up early Sunday morning and started the sixty-five mile drive in order to be at the rest stop on time. When I arrived, I could see Duke trudging up the side of the mountain from the camp in the valley.

My heart jumped, I was so glad to see him.

I was also scared that he might get caught or I might be sent to jail as an accomplice, but I was so excited it didn't matter. The danger, in fact, added to my excitement.

He jumped into the car and lay down on the floor. "Get goin', before they miss me."

When we were away from the camp area, he got up off the floor. "Hi ya, doll. Just keep driving."

"How do you know they won't miss you?"

"Guys do it all the time. It's almost like the guards turn their backs on the whole thing."

He grabbed me around the shoulders with one arm and started going for my thighs.

"Wait 'til I park the car!" I giggled.

"Oh, I missed my little girl. Turn here and head up that road. It takes us up into the woods."

I hated it when Duke called me "little girl." Even then, amidst all the excitement, I felt its sting. Sometimes I wished Duke would just not talk. All I wanted was his body.

I stopped the car, and we got out and walked until we came to some brush. He threw me down and kissed me wildly, a look in his eyes to match. I pulled off my pants. The brush was scratchy. Duke pulled off his pants and tried to go inside me, but his penis wasn't hard enough. He said they were putting something in the food at the camp, and then he ejaculated. I was glad. My whole back and backside were itching from brush scratches.

We talked and Duke said, "I guess you better take me back to the road. I'll go back to the camp, and then you can come through the gate at eleven for visiting hours."

I dropped him off, and he started his mile-long trek down the side of the mountain. I drove to the tree and masturbated while I waited for eleven.

At the front gate, the correctional officer called Duke and he ambled over. "Hi, honey. Haven't seen you in a long time."

We sat on the benches and again I was fascinated by the women visiting the other men in camp. I thought they must all be sick, putting up with men who are always in trouble with the law. Don't they realize they're playing mommy to all these losers? Why don't they just tell these guys to get lost? I thought I was different even though I knew I hadn't got what I wanted from Duke this trip.

While we were standing by my car, saying goodbye, one of the other inmates walked up and said, "If your wife is going back to San Diego, Duke, how about her giving my wife a ride?"

"How'd your wife get here?" Duke asked.

"She got a ride, but the girl left already."

I said I'd take his wife back and in a few minutes, the inmate and his wife came to the car carrying a cage. Duke opened the back of my station wagon, and they slid the cage in. I got behind the wheel, and the woman climbed in beside me. She was messed up. I wondered if she and her husband had had sex on the bench.

"Hi. My husband catches things for me up here. I keep them at the house."

I looked in my rearview mirror and staring right back at me were four round eyes that belonged to two very large owls. They stood side by side in the cage, like two soldiers ready for inspection.

I started the car and said goodbye to Duke.

About half an hour down the road, the woman spoke again.

"Owls eat live chickens."

I didn't have a quick answer. Curious, I finally asked, "What do you do with the owls?"

"We got all kinds of things around our house. Owls, snakes, rats, mice..."

"Must make nice pets."

We didn't speak again. I knew this lady had a screw loose somewhere, and I was afraid to push any of her buttons. I checked the rearview mirror again, and the owls had turned in unison and were now looking out the side window, together. In a few moments they had turned and were looking out the other window. The last time I checked, they were staring back at me through the mirror.

I dropped the lady off on the outskirts of San Diego in front of her house. She took the owl cage out of the wagon and said, "Remember, owls eat live chickens."

The day's experience didn't stop me from repeating the same performance four more times.

I learned to carry pillows and a blanket with me. One day we found a huge drainpipe and made a bed inside of it. Another day we lay by a beautiful stream, hidden away from the world, until a Boy Scout troop came marching past just as I was about to reach orgasm. As bizarre as it was—in spite of the money spent on gasoline, in spite of the danger and indignity if I were caught—these adventures in the mountains took me away from my problems and always thinking about money.

Lori decided to leave and go live with her sister in Santa Cruz. I didn't blame her. Anyone who could leave the kind of chaos our family lived in was crazy not to. I knew she would have helped me if she could. No one looking from the outside could have known what to do. I was on the inside, and I didn't know.

Soon after, Mary left Seth and moved in with me. Seth had been taking more and more drugs and told her once that he dreamed he killed her. His strange behavior frightened her, and she was about to have the baby. Seth was upset about her leaving, but he supported her financially. He thought she would come to her senses and return to him. When an apartment became available near me, Mary moved into it.

It was January 1968 when Seth called me at work and told me Mary was about to deliver her baby. By the time I arrived at the hospital, the baby had been born. I sat down next to Seth, who looked drawn and exhausted.

"Have they told you what we got?" I asked happily.

"No. The nurse said the doctor would be out in a minute, but it's been a long time."

Seth and I sat there, both with the feeling that something was wrong. I smelled beer on him. I had a very sensitive nose since I had stopped drinking. I had always considered Seth a fine artist, but his abuse of drugs worried me. I wanted my daughter to be happy and had supported her decision to leave Seth. Still, I understood his addiction and felt a kinship between us. I thought I might be able to help him, but I never did.

The doctor walked out from the delivery room and took off his mask. He was dead serious.

"Mary had a baby boy. I'm sorry to have to tell you this, but he was born with severe club feet. Mary is doing fine. I called in a specialist immediately for the baby. He broke both feet and straightened them out."

I was stunned, and Seth looked as though he would faint.

"When can we see her?"

"In a few minutes. You can see the baby now. He's in the nursery."

Seth and I looked through the window at the new tiny baby in the bassinet. The nurse pulled the covers back, and we saw the casts on both little legs. I cried, and Seth walked away.

After Seth came out of Mary's room, we said goodbye and it was my turn to go in. Mary was sitting up in bed, her black eyes shining.

"Don't worry, Mom. It'll be okay."

I kissed her. "I know it will, Mary. I'm so sorry."

"His name is Mark."

"I like that."

"The baby and I had a talk, and we know everything's going to be fine. We have faith."

I held back my tears.

On the way out, I met the doctor in the hall.

"What causes this to happen?"

"Ask Seth about the LSD he took," he answered in anger.

"Do you think that caused the club feet?"

"Yes, I do. These kids have gone crazy with these drugs!"

"Did you say anything to Seth?"

"I certainly did. It didn't seem to make any impression on him. He just hung his head and walked away."

"Do they have any proof that LSD causes birth defects?"

"I'll bet that's the cause of this one. I asked Mary if he had been on drugs, and she told me he had."

"My husband's sister had a baby with club feet, and I know they didn't take drugs."

"Maybe. I have another patient I have to see now." He stormed down the hall, and I left.

I never had got a straight answer from any doctor I had ever been to. The same doctor that delivered Mary's baby, our so-called family doctor, had told me a few years before that I had rheumatoid arthritis.

"No way am I going to accept that!" I told myself.

I was never bothered by it again.

I thought of the time I took Colleen to the Navy hospital to get a burr taken out of her foot. She was four. She cried and screamed on the table, so the doctor took a sheet and wrapped her up like a mummy so she couldn't move. I had seen the terror in her face as the doctor poked her foot, trying to get the burr out, but I hadn't moved to stop him. In those days, I thought the doctor was always right. He didn't get the burr out. Colleen pulled it out herself when we got home.

It took me a long time to see doctors for what they were. Just people mechanics, some good and some bad. During a pelvic examination, a doctor once tickled my cunt and asked me how it felt. I pretended it was a medical question although I knew it wasn't. Another doctor had told me my bladder needed repair because I had had so many children.

"I can just tie it up and take a few stitches. That will sure make the men happy."

"I don't want that operation," I said.

"You'll be sorry when you start to wet your pants when you sneeze."

That was 24 years ago, and I haven't wet my pants yet.

I wondered if I had really needed a hysterectomy at thirty-six, or if the Navy doctors had decided to stop me from having so many children.

I hoped the doctor who had taken care of Mark's feet was a good one. I went home from the hospital feeling as though my life were a giant puzzle with the pieces scattered everywhere. I had no idea what the picture was. When I divorced Karl and became sober, I had great hopes. How naive I had been.

Mary brought Mark home to her apartment. I found her standing at her kitchen sink, three weeks later, with her tiny baby immersed in water. Mary was in tears.

I took hold of the baby and saw that his casts were half on and half off.

"The doctor said I had to soak the casts off. He said Mark is too little to saw them off. But I can't get them off!"

"Let's go slow. Maybe we can do it together. I don't know why they left this for you to do."

"I don't either. I can't do it. I just can't. It scares me."

We finally managed to get the casts off. Mary had to wait two days for Mark's legs to "dry out" before she took him back to the doctor for new casts. She took the baby to the doctor once a week for six months. Mark was in hip casts, knee casts, and finally braces that wouldn't allow him to move at night.

The baby's crying almost drove Mary crazy. I supported her as much as I could, but I had to go to work every day. I couldn't miss a beat, or we would all be in trouble.

Mary began making artificial flowers to sell and was learning to accept her situation. What she had said in the hospital had been right; she had faith that the baby would be okay, and I saw in her the kind of inner strength I hadn't even found in myself yet.

Seth went into the Army. He made arrangements for Mary to get an allotment check, and that made her feel secure.

My money problems were endless. It was time for school clothes again. The summer had been easier on my budget, but I hadn't saved anything for the new school year. Money went out as fast as I earned it. I asked myself if I was handling my money right, but I knew I hadn't wasted a penny.

When I phoned the District Attorney's office, which I did often, they said they were working on my problem. Karl had moved so many times, it was hard to keep up with him. I was positive that if Karl would only pay the child-support money on time every month, I could get organized. I hated waiting for checks that never arrived or partial payments that came late.

One Saturday morning I woke to see the landlord painting just outside my bedroom window. Alarmed, I asked what had made him decide to paint the trolley station. Was he getting ready to sell it?

"No," he said. "It just needs painting. I'm not going to sell it."

About a week later, his wife came to the door to tell me I would have to move. They had sold the house, and the new owners wanted us out. We had thirty days.

The children and I were crushed. We had all fallen in love with this grand old building, and we had been happy on the beach. We all looked for another place close by, but nothing that we could afford was available.

I found a house across Mission Bay in a modest middle-class neighborhood. The rent was $165, which was $35 more than I had been paying each month. I decided to take the chance, and we started packing.

I was busy packing in the livingroom, when I heard Colleen calling from out front.

"What do you want?"

"Look! There's Spot flying around the front door."

"What are you talking about?"

"The butterfly! My pet butterfly. I named her Spot."

"Oh, pretty," I said.

"She rides around on my handlebars with me."

"Come on, Colleen. I'm trying to pack so we can move."

"Please, Mom. Just watch a minute! Please!"

Impatient, I watched. In a few seconds the butterfly flew to the handlebars of Colleen's bike and stayed there while she rode up and down the sidewalk in front of the house.

When she stopped, Spot flew back and fluttered around the front door.

"See? What'd I tell you?"

"That's really interesting," I mused. I had to believe it. I saw it.

"She's been my pet for a long time. She loves me."

An affectionate butterfly was a tiny miracle. It made me happy for the rest of that day.

THE
YELLOW
HOUSE

The yellow house was an old tract house with three bedrooms, a two-and-a-half car garage, a small front yard, and a large back yard with a patio. Bird of Paradise plants, shrubs, flowers, two tall palm trees and a prickly oriental tree in the back decorated the unpretentious house. I felt it had housed caring people at one time.

Steve, David and Tim got a U-Haul, and we moved all our junky old furniture into the new house. I put an old bedspread over the exposed springs and threadbare upholstery of the couch, and we fixed things up as best we could.

I bought a doberman puppy for Colleen, my animal lover, and the dog was happy in the fenced-in back yard.

As soon as Duke got out of the honor camp, he came right to the house. Why couldn't he have been here to help us move, I wondered.

"Star isn't a good name for that dog," Duke exclaimed.

"It's the name Colleen chose. We like it."

"She should have a name like Princess or something."

"Damn it, her name is Star!"

Duke tried to make a contribution. When I got home from work one day, he had spent the entire day weeding and trimming the yard. It looked great. I hugged his sweaty, dirty body in thanks. I knew he wanted to feel he belonged and was trying to make me accept him again.

Duke was sleeping in his mother's garage. He had a comfortable bed in the corner but sacks of manure for the yard were stacked up in the other corner. His mother didn't trust him any longer to stay sober and didn't want him in her house. When he got a job as a used-car salesman, however, she bought him suits and other clothes to wear on the job. Between Mrs. Ellsworth and me, Duke had two mothers.

The three boys wanted to move into the big garage. They promised to fix it up and take care of it. Old rugs were put down, posters were put up all over the walls and garage beams, and a cheap stereo, candles, incense, books, magazines, albums, pictures of Jimmy and Janis and the Moody Blues, and a stolen Laguna Beach City Limits sign were scattered lovingly around. As a less important item, beds were added.

A lot of people lived in garages on Mission Beach. The kids loved it. They were still part of the family but independent. I called them the Garage People.

I was working extremely hard on my job. The boys were always off somewhere, and it was impossible for me to keep track of them. Susan helped me with the house, and Colleen pitched in when asked. She had the entire care of Star and was doing a great job. The neighbors weren't unfriendly. They got a kick out of Colleen pulling Star along the sidewalk by a leash.

My grocery bill was climbing and I seemed to be spending most of my time away from work at the supermarket. I was still fighting with the District Attorney over locating Karl.

Every weekend Duke would drive up in a different car and expound on the huge amounts of money he was going to make. His fantasies were real to him, but it wasn't long before he was drunk again. This time they put him in the County Mental Health Hospital.

No matter what went on around me, I continued to work on my writing each night. Mary especially liked one of my plays and told me to send it in to a play contest being held at one of the colleges.

"Mary, that play has been rejected twenty times."

"I don't care. I like it. Will you send it in for me?"

"I think it's a waste of time, but I'll send it."

One day I got a phone call at work. I was sure it was a bill collector.

"Miss Hall? This is Mr. Mires at Grossmont College. I want to congratulate you. Your play *Lost* won the contest and the fifty dollar prize."

"I won? Yippee! I won the play contest!"

The whole office turned around and grinned.

"We're going to produce your play and are having tryouts Monday evening. Can you be there?"

"Oh, yes. I'll be there."

"At the theater at seven."

"Oh, thank you, thank you!"

I was so excited I didn't know what I was doing. I told everyone I knew about my victory. At last, my secret night work, my secret self, would be public and validated. I wanted to shout to the world, "I exist! I exist!"

Working, paying bills, trying to feed the children, fixing bodies, fixing cars, getting love from Duke, dealing with the school system, fighting for child support—all were interwoven with my stolen hours of writing each night. What had kept me going with no encouragement all these years? Somewhere inside me I dreamed of making money as a writer and getting away from the corporations, where I knew I would never go very high up the men's ladder. I was often full of doubts about my writing, especially when I read other authors. They were artists, and I felt I was only a reporter. But I knew I was a good reporter and had a sense of drama. I felt people needed to share honest stories of struggle. Writing gave me a dream.

I went to the tryouts, and for the first time since I ice-skated as a teenager, I felt worthwhile. It was my play. I had written it, and it had nothing to do with being a mother, being divorced, being a slave to the corporation, being an alcoholic, being middle-aged, or being some man's wife or girlfriend. I felt like a person.

By the time we had moved into the yellow house, I had learned not to expect anything from Duke. He never came around drunk, but sometimes he would call drunk, and I would hang up. When he was sober, I allowed him back into my life for lovemaking and fun-time. I had accepted the fact that I would never have a permanent life with Duke. We were too different. I wanted to win.

Duke was in the hospital—his third mother—but I wanted him to see my play. I called him up, and he said he could get a pass for special occasions.

"I really want to see it, doll."

"I'll pick you up Friday night at seven."

"I'm sure I can go."

"Oh, Duke, I can't believe it's happening!"

The play was running Friday, Saturday, and Sunday for two weekends. Chris was coming to San Diego for the second weekend to go with his brothers and sisters.

I planned to attend every performance, but I wanted Duke to be with me for the first one, to share my excitement.

I was really high when I drove to pick up Duke. He was waiting outside, all dressed up, looking like a man of distinction. I was bubbling over to think he was going to share this with me. He got into the car, and I started off down the busy street.

"I'm so excited," I babbled. "All the San Diego reviewers will be there, Duke."

"Jesus, I feel awful," Duke said in a flat voice. "They got me doped up or something."

I wasn't sympathetic. "Just pretend you feel good, Duke. Just for me."

"Shut up, damn it! I suppose those newspaper guys will be there too," he accused.

Suddenly I recalled Duke's reaction to a news article about me, run a few weeks earlier in connection with the play. He had resented it. Duke was jealous of anyone's success, but especially mine. And he didn't like anyone else to pay attention to me, especially the news media.

I swallowed my anger. "Please, Duke. Calm down. It's going to be all right. You'll have a good time."

"Don't tell me to calm down. Jesus Christ! Let me out of this car!"

I jammed on the brakes, nosing in by the curb. "Okay, get out! You wouldn't give me even one lousy night without acting like an ass! Get out and stay out!"

He got out of the car, screaming at me. "You dumb bitch! You're crazier than any dumb bitch I ever knew!"

I pushed on the gas and tore off. I could smell the tires. I looked into the rear view mirror. Duke was storming down the street in the direction of the hospital. Would he make it? It was only six blocks away. I couldn't worry about it. I was determined to let nothing spoil my opening night.

I sat in the middle of the theater so I could watch the audience. The curtain opened, and my heart pounded. There before me were my own characters come to life. They were exactly as I had imagined them. I was deeply moved by the actors' efforts and thought of the director and others who had brought my play to life.

As the play continued, I watched the faces in the audience. They liked it! When it was over, they clapped with enthusiasm. I walked outside, and someone said to me, "Wasn't that a great play?"

I laughed happily. "I'm the author."

"You are? Wow! Hey, this is the author!"

The college students gathered around me and told me how much they liked my play. I was happy they understood it. It was about lack of communication between people.

I showed up at each performance. I went backstage and thanked the students who were in it. I never thought about Duke during the entire run of the play.

When Chris and Lori arrived in San Diego, the whole family went to the play together. It was a treat, having my children all together and entertaining them in such a new way.

Chris said, "Gee, Mom, I didn't know you could write like that!"

"What do you think I've been doing for the past nine years?"

The other children said they thought I was just dreaming, that they had never taken my typing seriously. To them, I was just Mom, struggling to pay the bills.

All of my life until now I had been at the bottom of the canyon trying to crawl out. That evening I was at the top of the mountain touching the rainbow.

Susan was fourteen and had not menstruated. I was getting worried.

I made an appointment with Dr. Root, but when we got to the office, he wasn't in. He was out flying his airplane. Dr. Burton was taking his patients.

The nurse called Susan into the examination room for her first pelvic examination. In a few minutes, Dr. Burton came out to the waiting room to get me. We went to the exam table and just stood there. The doctor was disturbed, and his hands were shaking.

"I'm sorry to have to tell you this, Mrs. Hall, but Susan has no vagina."

"She what?"

"Well, she looks perfectly normal from the outside and I guess that's what shocked me when I tried to examine her."

"Is that why no one ever noticed?"

"I'm sure of it."

My mind was racing frantically. "What causes it?"

He wiped his forehead with a handkerchief. "We're not sure but she was born that way. It happens every once in a while. I'm sorry."

He shook his head and, not wanting a scene, politely walked me to the door.

I felt sick inside. I took a deep breath and tried to compose myself to face Susan, who was waiting in the car.

"What's wrong with me?" she asked.

I looked at my beautiful Susan sitting beside me.

"You're perfectly healthy," I said. "But you were born without a vagina."

She didn't quite understand, for which I was grateful. I kept on talking, trying to keep my sense of tragedy out of my voice.

"When you meet a nice boy some day, there will be ways you can make love with a man anyway. When you're older, I'll explain. Right now, the important thing is that you're perfectly healthy, with or without your period."

She gave me a long look. "Oh well, I didn't want to mess around with periods anyway." She was thoughtful. "Then I'm not really a slow learner? And if we tell them this will they let me out of the special classes?"

I smiled as I saw the connection in her mind and realized that getting out of the special classes was much more important to her than the lack of a vagina.

"Damn right I'm getting you out. Right now!"

I called Mrs. Houseman the next day.

"I want Susan out of the special class and in the regular ninth grade. Immediately."

"But, Mrs. Hall..."

"Mrs. Houseman, it's Miss Hall. And this time I mean what I'm saying."

"Are you sure you're doing the right thing? I mean, what if she fails?"

"I'm going to give her that chance. She needs and wants the regular classes, and I've made up my mind. Will you please get her transferred?"

"Well, if that's your decision."

"It is. And, Mrs. Houseman, thank you for all the help you've given Susan. We both appreciate it very much."

"She's a lovely young girl, you know."

"Yes, I know, Mrs. Houseman. Thank you."

Susan went into the ninth grade the last half of that semester and on to high school the following year. She was so happy to be going to regular classes, and about her life in general, that we didn't talk about her physical problem again for a long time.

Tim was working at the Waffle Shop and had bought a car. He also had a new guitar and was buying secondhand musical sound equipment. Things were happening in the garage. He and his friends were practicing and putting on rock-and-roll concerts for the whole family.

Strange kids would knock on the front door and ask for Tim and David. I directed them to the garage. Out there, Tim, David and Steve were running their own lives. Once in a while, I still yelled at them when they caused a disturbance inside the house, but it seemed ludicrous to yell up at a six-footer, which two of them had become.

Tim was graduating from high school that year and was very serious about his music. He practiced all the time, wrote songs, and was becoming a very good musician. Politics were changing, long hair ruled, and everyone was participating in or at least aware of the new Hippie movement. Parents were going crazy with all the changes, and the kids kept right on shocking them.

David was suspended from school for smoking a cigarette in the gym. I was slowly becoming aware of the system's shortcomings, and sympathized more and more with my children's boredom with classes.

David was especially bitter and disillusioned with school. I knew it even though he stopped showing his frustrations and disappointments. The last one he told me about was his experience in drama class. He had spent the previous summer-school semester enthusiastically learning stage-craft with real professionals, and had earned an A in the class. In the regular drama class during the fall, however, when he had tried to share his experiences and ideas with the class and teacher, he was closed out. I wanted to go yell at the teacher, to tell her how important this interest was to David, but David wouldn't let me. I understood, and I watched him get deeper and deeper into drugs.

Steve at twelve was growing like a weed. He was still building bicycles from spare parts, sometimes even selling one. I didn't think he was using drugs, but marijuana was available in the garage any time he wanted to start. I talked frequently to the three boys about drugs, but they always lied to me about it to avoid trouble. There wasn't much I could say without sounding like a reformed addict. My example was the best advice I could give them, but it was torture not being able to pass on my experience.

At work, the drug problem was even worse. It seemed as if everyone had pills. The young people used speed, and the older men had drawers full of tranquilizers and an unbelievable number of medications. I suddenly realized I wasn't the only one unhappy working for the corporation. Each person there wanted to be doing something else with his or her life. Our supervisor was a whip-cracking martinet. Yet, he gained nothing for the company in increased output, for all the misery he caused the workers.

Tim turned eighteen, and it was his time to sign up for the draft. We sat down to talk about it.

"I don't want you to go to Vietnam," I said, "but I don't know about going to Canada."

"I don't know either," said Tim. "Let's just wait and see if I get called. Maybe they'll stop this shit before they get to me."

When Duke was sober and came to visit, we got into horrible battles over the war. After I went to a peace march, I didn't think he would ever shut up. He thought I was crazy. I couldn't believe his hypocrisy. He had done everything he could, in the navy and out, to upset the establishment and disobey the law. He had an uncanny ability to avoid work. He griped about the police incessantly. He lived off his mother or a mother-substitute every day of his life. And still he thought of himself as a great patriot.

I guessed supporting war was part of the John Wayne image so many losers like Duke have. He was a brawling, hard-drinking, tough-talking, woman-fucking stiff who defended the flag, mother, and the American way—and hated all of them.

The next year, 1969, I submitted another play to the college contest, and once again I won first prize. This time the check was for one hundred and fifty dollars.

The children now took me seriously when I asked them to be quiet so I could write. It had taken me a long time to learn the difference between a male and female writer: a man was at work, but a woman was self indulgent.

My success encouraged me to continue working on my autobiography. I resisted any temptation to involve Duke in my success this time. I decided it was mine to enjoy, myself.

One Saturday morning I went to the garage to do the washing. Tim was still sleeping although it was time for him to go to work. When I woke him, he screamed at me in an almost insane voice.

"Don't tell me what to do! Get rid of that goddamn bum, Duke. I hate him. He's not your kind. He's a stupid asshole. I hate that drunken bastard."

"What's wrong with you?" I yelled back.

"Just get out of here and leave me alone."

"Sorry, but you'll have to wait until I get the wash in."

I was shocked and hurt, but underneath I knew he was right. Why couldn't I tell Duke I didn't want to see him again? What was this insane idea I had that the bad guys were exciting? I remembered that as a little girl, my favorite movie had been *Algiers*. Maybe I still saw myself as Hedy Lamarr, running through the Casbah trying to find Pepe Le Moko.

Tim's draft notice came in the mail. He decided to go and get it over with.

I was sick, scared, and full of guilt. I didn't know what to tell him to do. If I had known someone important and influential, would that have helped him? If I had more money and had sent him to college, would that have made him safe from Vietnam?

Tim spent his waiting time getting drunk and stoned. He was hung over when the taxi arrived at six a.m. to take him to the bus depot and basic training. I got up and helped him get his things together.

"Will you send me my guitar later?"

"Sure I will, Tim."

He put everything into the cab and came back to kiss me.

"Mom, I don't want to die."

"I know, Tim. I'll pray that you don't have to go to Vietnam. I love you."

"I love you too, Mom. See ya."

I watched the cab drive away, the tears rolling down my face. Back in the house, everyone was still asleep, and I sat on the metal springs of the couch and hardly felt them. I could figure out no better way to fight this monstrous wrong than anything else that had happened to me. I wanted to fight back. I wanted to scream. All I could do was cry.

Tim wrote me from Fort Hood, Texas, as soon as he arrived:

Dear Mom,
Camp is really neat!! The counselor takes us on hikes every day! Wish you were here!

your loving son,
Timothy

I tried to put Tim out of my mind, for the next six weeks anyway. Susan and David were an immediate concern. Susan's problems were actually in my mind. She was doing great in school.

Now in the tenth grade, she studied her heart out, and her life took on a new freshness. However, it wasn't long before I found out that the other kids in her high school were ignoring her. She had a label, "special class," and that made her different. She said she didn't mind, but I was sure she must. Nevertheless, she kept on studying and pretending. Whenever I got depressed, I watched how she accepted life and her fate, and I was ashamed of myself.

When she brought home passing grades, her eyes were shining. "See, I told you I could do it, Mom."

"That's really great, Susan. I'm sorry I didn't get you into regular classes when you first said you could do it. I should have believed you."

Because she was such a good kid, and didn't demand as much attention as the other children, I seldom took time to talk to Susan as much as she deserved. I knew she was doing fine, and gave my attention to other problems.

David was a roving bomb. He never sat down and was constantly in trouble. He was completely soured on school and quit after the eleventh grade. He had a heart murmur and that worried me, but I was happy when he was away from home. He was into drugs and in constant trouble with the law.

Juvenile Hall phoned me one evening and told me to come get him.

When I walked into that horrible place and saw all those young people—mostly minority kids—locked up, I shuddered. David came walking down the hall.

"Mom, get me out of this place."

"What am I going to do with you when I get you out?" I asked coldly. "You won't listen to me. You're no good to yourself or the family the way you're acting."

"You wouldn't leave me, would you?" He started to cry and so did I. We went home, and things were quiet for a time.

One night he said to me, "I'm going to the beach."

I looked on his belt where he had a knife in a case. It really scared me. "You're not going out of this house with that knife!"

"Yes I am! There's nothing wrong with carrying a knife. It's legal if it's out in the open. I'm going."

I grabbed him. "Like hell you are! Give me that knife!"

I was raving, envisioning him flipping out on drugs and hurting someone with his violent temper and high energy.

"Stay back, Mom. Now stop it."

We wrestled. "Give me that knife or I'll call the police!"

He took the knife out but held on to it.

"Here, see. It's just a small one."

In desperation, I grabbed the knife and put it on the antique family Bible that someone had given me.

"There now! Take your pick. Either the Bible or the knife."

"You're crazy," he said, but he left the knife as he walked out the door.

It *was* crazy. I felt as if I'd acted out a scene from Father Flannagan's *Boy's Town*. I didn't get much satisfaction out of my encounters with David. He sought his own answers.

Colleen graduated from sixth grade and was on her way to junior high. She always brought home good report cards and had a best girlfriend who lived down the street. Her brothers and sisters thought she was spoiled. It was true that I treated her differently.

By the time Colleen was out of childhood, I saw that all the screaming and shouting had been useless, even harmful, to the other children. The only time I yelled at her was when I thought her life or somebody else's was in danger. It worked fine. She taught herself all the lessons she needed to know.

When she was four and Karl was still living with us, we had an old refrigerator out on the patio to keep extra milk in. Colleen was playing with our cat Murphy on the patio and decided he would like to play inside the refrigerator. That night we called and called but no Murphy. Colleen especially called and was upset when he didn't come home. The next morning I found Murphy refrigerator-cold dead. We had a very somber funeral up on the hill, marking Murphy's grave with a cross of popsicle sticks.

Colleen's care of our dog, Star, was devoted.

One day, I came home from work, and Colleen said, "Guess who came to visit us!"

"Who?" I asked.

"Spot."

"Oh, come on now, Colleen, I'm tired."

"No, honest, Mom. He's in the bathroom. Come on, I'll show you."

We went into the bathroom and, sure enough, there was a butterfly that looked just like Spot. He flew onto Colleen's shoulder and stayed there until she walked outside.

"It can't be the same one. Clear across the bay. Besides, butterflies have short lifespans."

"Mom, I tell you, it is Spot."

David tried to get into one of the services. He was rejected because of his heart murmur. He worked at several jobs and roamed the beach. When I asked him why in the world he wanted to join the military, he said he didn't know what else to do. I tried to talk him into going to junior college, which is free in California, but he wasn't interested in any more school.

One incredible day, David came home with some other young people. When I invited them into the house, David said, "Mom, I've just joined the Children of God."

"You've *what*?"

"I want you to meet Isaiah and Jeremiah."

"Hi, I'm glad to meet you," I said.

"Come see the bus I'm going on, Mom," said David happily. "It's at the beach."

"You're going away?"

"It's okay, Mom. Really. Just follow us."

I followed their old car to the beach and, sure enough, there was the bus. The young people motioned to me to come inside, and when I stepped into the bus, I saw about twenty kids. They were singing Jesus songs—not the usual hymns, but songs that were peppy. One boy was playing the guitar, and the others were passing around a tray of bread. I took a piece and chewed away.

Jeremiah sat down beside me. "We're the Children of God. We are living by God's Holy Word. We see the sin in the system, and we choose to live according to the Bible."

"Right on," I said agreeably.

"David has made his decision to go with us."

"Oh?"

"We have a commune in Texas, and we travel around picking up lost souls everywhere."

He told me they had picked David up, wandering on the beach, loaded on LSD. I looked at the other kids. They appeared to be clean and sober.

David was singing and happy, still loaded. I asked him to step outside the bus so I could talk to him.

"This is NOT what I had in mind the other night when I put the knife on the Bible!"

"This has nothing to do with that, Mom. But these people are really neat!"

"Are you clear-headed enough to know what you're doing? Is this really what you want?"

"Mom, I'm sure."

I thought about his alternatives: boredom, restlessness, drugs, trouble with the police.

"Well, I can't stop you," I sighed.

He was happy as a kid. "Say, Mom, do you have any old clothes or blankets we could have? Like it says in the Bible, I'm supposed to give all my material possessions to them."

They weren't going to get much out of David or me, I thought. "I guess I could find a few things."

"We'll come by and pick them up."

As I went through the old clothes and junk I had saved over the years, I thought of all the secondhand clothes people had given me when the children were small. Boxes of children's clothes, full of holes and worn out. I hadn't wanted to be ungrateful, but my kids already *had* wornout clothes. I had vowed then I would never pass along anything that wasn't in good shape. The things I gave to the Children of God, however, were pretty awful.

When David and the boys came by the house, they praised me to high heaven for the junk. Their talk was full of Bible quotations. I thought, well, it was good practice in humility to be joyful over so little. At forty-five, I was cynical about "joining" anything for easy answers. Also, I had never liked being told what to do. I thought David and the Children of God had a lot to learn.

I kissed David goodbye and prayed he was doing the right thing.

My company didn't get another contract, and I was laid off again. I spent the first few days sleeping and being depressed. Then I decided it was a perfect time to work on my book, which I had neglected lately.

Almost every week I called the District Attorney's office to see how my case was coming, and I always got the same answer:

"We're working on it."

I couldn't help thinking of what all the other abandoned mothers did who didn't have my drafting skill to pay the bills while the DA's office "worked on it." Went on welfare, probably. It was hard for me to imagine how a father could cut himself off from the care of his children. Yet Karl was one of thousands, maybe millions.

When Duke came over, we would have sex and then argue during the rest of our time together. We didn't seem to have anything at all in common anymore except sex. Maybe I was just recognizing that we never had anything in common. He had never offered to help the family financially or any other way, except at odd moments, when he would do something like trim the yard. I was bored. After we fucked, I wanted him to leave.

He was still living in his mother's garage, and I couldn't understand why a grown man would want to live with his mother.

"What if your mother finds another man to marry?" I asked.

"She wouldn't do that. She doesn't care anything about men."

"Really, Duke, you're incredible! Don't you think your mother has any sexuality?"

"She's sixty-five years old, dummy. She doesn't care about that anymore."

"Sixty-five isn't old."

"Jesus, is that all you think about—sex? Just leave my mother alone."

"When are *you* going to leave her alone!"

"I'm leaving. I'm going to Arizona. After I get settled and find a job, I'll send for you and the kids."

Not a chance, I thought to myself.

"Listen, Nancy, I'm sick of this whole town. The cops are after me all the time, just waiting to lock me up again. I need some peace of mind."

I was no longer interested in his problems. Or his plans. My peace of mind was more important to me than his.

The phone rang. It was Tim calling collect from Fort Hood, Texas.

"I've been busted by the CID, Mom. The legal officer is a guy from California, and he's cool. He's trying to get me out of here because I have my orders for Vietnam."

"What happened?"

"They claim I sold some pot to an agent in Kileen. Some punk kid in the army, seventeen years old, wants to be a CID agent."

"What do you want me to do?"

"Call the legal officer. His name is Lt. Joe Pearce."

"Where did you get arrested?"

"In Kileen. So the county of Kileen is pressing charges too. Do you know what the sentence is in Texas for drugs? Life in prison. This place is the pits."

Oh, Mother God.

"They already had me in an interrogation room asking me questions. Then the legal officer told me to get my shit together and get ready to leave here. I have thirty days leave if I can get out of here."

"Okay, Tim, I'll call the legal officer. Call me again as soon as you can."

When I hung up the phone, I was shaking worse than I ever had from a hangover. I phoned Lt. Pearce. He said he was hoping to get Tim's orders signed right away but advised me to get a lawyer in California to fight extradition. I said I would immediately and for him to please call me when Tim got out of Texas.

I called my lawyer, who immediately phoned Lt. Pearce for the details of the case. I was in a panic. Prison in Texas! Life! Did they want to make an example of Tim? Just for marijuana? What kinds of games were they up to?

I couldn't sleep that night. The next morning I got a call from Lt. Pearce in Texas.

"He got out of here, and he's on his way home for his leave. He'd better get in contact with his lawyer right away because the CID is still after him. He just made it out."

"Lieutenant Pearce, thank you so much for your help. I can't thank you enough."

"That's okay. Good luck."

When Tim got home, we went directly to the lawyer. He told Tim that when his leave was up and he went to Oakland to get shipped out to Vietnam, he should put in a call to me every night at eight o'clock, and the first night I didn't get the call, I was to contact the lawyer immediately.

Later, Tim told me the details of his escape.

"I packed my gear, went to the sergeant to get my papers signed, and he said, 'Wait, there's a note here that I have to check with the CID office before I sign your papers.' He dialed the CID office, and it rang about eight times. He couldn't get an answer, so he said, 'Fuck it, get out of here.' The CID was behind me all the way to the airport, but I made it onto the plane."

"Will they bother you on leave?"

"I don't think so."

Tim spent his leave with his friends and then left for Oakland. The first night he phoned at exactly eight and each night after that. Each night I sat by the phone and prayed.

"Mother God, please let Tim get to Vietnam!" Oh, the irony!

Tim's first letter from Vietnam said: "They really wanted me for the war, Mom. They got me out of the bust and into the war just like they wanted. More hamburger meat!"

My worries were like the chicken pox. By the time I had the last sore scratched, the first one itched again.

Chris and Lori had a little boy and were living in Moss Beach, near Santa Cruz. Chris was out of the Air Force and working as an electrician. Lori was pregnant again.

Mary was living in Ocean Beach with Mark and working at the Waffle Shop. Seth got an emergency leave to try and get back together with her, and Mary went to bed with him. Now she was pregnant. They didn't get back together, and Mary decided she and Mark would move in with me.

Tim's and my letters went back and forth across the Pacific, and every time Tim's arrived, I read it with the fear that it was his last.

Steve was occupying the garage, playing the stereo and practicing with his drum sticks on boxes. I missed the live music and "I'm So Glad," the piece they played over and over before Tim left for Vietnam.

Steve dug up half the back yard and planted corn. It was about a foot high when I noticed the birds were eating it.

"You'd better build a scarecrow, Steve, or they'll eat it all up," I suggested.

I went out looking for a job, and when I returned late in the afternoon, Steve had made a scarecrow. It was about four feet tall, had on an old, long-sleeved, green-flannel shirt, grubby khaki pants. A volley ball was the head and a big photograph of Nixon was pasted on the ball. The arms were stretched up and out, and the mittens on the arms were sewed into Vs. In one hand was a sign that read: "I am your scarecrow, make no mistake about that!"

I laughed and laughed. The neighbors laughed. Someone called the newspaper and a photographer came out the next day and took a picture. It was on the front page, and Steve was a star—with some people.

A few days later I received a letter in the mail:

Dear Mrs. Hall:

What a dreadful thing to let your child do. You should take his wet diaper off and give him a thorough spanking. I raised three children to respect their president, Democrat or Republican. What can we expect of our children with such parents as you? I did not vote for Nixon but I mean to stick by him while he's trying to do his best (not make a scarecrow out of him). I wonder what would happen to him in one of the iron curtain countries.

From a good citizen and proud of our country and the right to vote for who we like.

Mrs. D

What Mrs. D didn't know—and I didn't know either—was that Steve hadn't really enjoyed the publicity. He had been very nervous that the news photographer might get his pot plants in the picture.

Some time later, I decided to weed the garden. I pulled up the four-foot pot plants and stacked them in a pile with the rest of the weeds. Steve waited until I went into the house and then confiscated his marijuana crop.

How could I have been so dumb? It was because I had the chicken pox.

When Mary went into labor, I drove her to the hospital. I sat with her in the labor room: the bed was steel, the door was shut so that we could neither hear nor see any human activity.

"It's spooky in here," Mary said.

"Like a science fiction laboratory," I agreed.

"There's no use in your staying, Mom. It may be a long time."

"I wouldn't leave you alone here."

We laughed. "At least go get yourself some coffee."

After a few hours, they told us to go home. It was false labor. The baby was two weeks late, and the second time we made sure we got to our own hospital. Mary's doctor came, checked her, and left. When it was time for her to go to the delivery room, he wasn't available. They called in another doctor.

I stood outside the delivery room and looked through the window.

Mary was screaming. The doctor looked worried and so did the nurses. What was the matter? Did the baby have club feet again? Or worse? I couldn't stand it. I went to the waiting section to sit.

"The baby is normal, and both are fine. It's a boy."

"Can I see Mary?" It was the only question I wanted to ask him.

Mary lay in her bed exhausted.

"What the hell happened in there? Are you all right?"

"Oh, Mom, it was awful. The spinal didn't take. I wasn't prepared. Everybody seemed to panic. I was scared."

I kissed her, not saying what I was thinking about doctors.

"Go to sleep now. Get some rest. It's all over."

"At least Matthew's fine. He's healthy. That's all I care about now."

Birth is a natural process, I was thinking. There must be a better, more satisfying way for a woman to deliver her baby than this.

A letter came in the mail from David. The envelope had a return address reading "Children of God, American Soul Clinic Youth Ranch, California." David had written on the envelope: "Jesus saith unto Him. I am the way, I am truth and the life—Jn. 14. 6."

On the back of the envelope flap was a little printed message: "Please send postage stamps."

Dear Nancy,

God bless you. Jesus really loves you. I really love you. I've been pretty busy doing what the Lord wants me to do and I'm very happy. I would like to know what you are reading of the bible and if you have any questions, send them to me. I'll ask the Lord to help me answer them for you. Really, I'm serious. I'm really praying for all of you out there, that you will come and see, it's so beautiful, I really love Jesus. He set me free and took care of all my problems and gave me the truth to spread throughout all the world. Please write.

Jezreel

I sent Jezreel some postage stamps in my next letter.

When Mary brought Matt home from the hospital, he cried continuously. He drove us all crazy, and when Mary finally took him to the doctor, the doctor said Matt was hyperactive. He suggested paregoric.

As far as I was concerned, it was that horrible birth that caused him to be so unhappy.

Mary was helping me pay the bills with her allotment check from Seth. Living on unemployment was impossible, and the District Attorney's office was still "working on it." I was out looking for work every day. The contracts just weren't coming into San Diego, they said. I would try to get as much information as I could over the phone to find out if an interview was worth spending gas money on before I went.

Mary and I were doing the washing one day.

"I hate to wash and iron," I said, "but I love to hang out the clothes on the line. Especially on a day like this."

"Be my guest," Mary laughed and went into the house to answer her baby's cry.

I pulled a shirt out of the basket, picked up a clothes pin, and was putting it on the shirt when a butterfly landed on the pin.

"Hello, Spot," I laughed. I kept on hanging clothes, and the butterfly kept on landing on my clothespins. When I was finished, the butterfly landed on my shoulder.

I went into the house and showed Mary. She knew Colleen's story about Spot.

"Maybe Spot's trying to tell you something."

"Maybe she's a reincarnation."

"Who's dead that loved you the most?"

"My grandma."

"She's saying hello and that she's with you."

"Thank you, Spot," I murmured as the butterfly fluttered off. "I needed that message." ·

Duke left for Arizona.

My sexual security was gone! I was forty-six, and I was afraid no man would ever love me again. I didn't love Duke, but without him I was lonely.

I told him I would write. He insisted that this time he would make it and send for me. I knew it was a fantasy, but at least he had moved away from his mother.

Now I was writing letters to Duke in Arizona, to David at the American Soul Clinic Youth Ranch, to Tim in Vietnam via San Francisco, and I was working on my book. Being unemployed made it easier to do all this writing but my money situation was bad. I couldn't get it out of my mind.

I hadn't attended AA meetings while I was going with Duke. I had lost touch with many of my close friends. When he left, I got back into the mainstream. I found comfort in being with AA people again.

I was sober. I worked hard, on the job and off. I faced my responsibilities. I paid my bills and, when I couldn't, I made the necessary adjustments with the bill collectors. The kids were well and happy—Mary with her babies, Susan with school, Steve with his projects, Colleen with Star. We had a roof over us and food on the table.

Nevertheless, a piece of me was missing.

One afternoon, Mother Goddess took me by the neck and sat me down in front of the television set.

Two young women were being interviewed. They were talking about Women's Liberation and invited women from all over San Diego to come to State College for a women's meeting on Wednesday night. I knew I would be attending that meeting. I knew nothing about the group but I sensed it was what I wanted.

I got in my car Wednesday night and drove to the college. I walked into the meeting and sat down among the fifty women. When we started talking, I felt instantly at home. We discussed housewives, welfare mothers, underpaid working women, single mothers, the Peace Movement, and even architecture. The energy among us was electric.

"I thought when I divorced Karl," I told them, "all I had to do was take my freedom. I was wrong. I ran smack up against poverty and lack of a place in the male world. Freedom came to me in little pieces."

They all knew what I was talking about.

Another woman spoke. "When my husband left me, I went into a depression for a year. He had been cheating on me and beating on me and kids for years, yet still I wanted to keep him. My family wanted me to keep him too. They said it wasn't too bad, men were like that."

I remembered something else. "I couldn't have made it without AA, its philosophy and the people there, but I got pretty upset when I heard a man say 'I can't stand the meetings where women talk about their monthly periods.' "

"Right on," the women agreed. "But if a man lost his job and the stress of that made it hard to be sober, he could tell about that, right?"

I knew I'd never be the same again. The chrysalis was breaking open, and the butterfly was about to appear.

After the meeting, the ten women from the community, who were not students, got together and formed a "rap group" of our own. We would meet every Thursday night at each others' houses, and the college women would share their literature with us.

Those meetings were different in every way from the coffee drinking sessions I had had with Navy wives, bitching and griping about our husbands. They were

105

deadly serious, yet full of laughter and joy, with discovery. We dug down into the dark places of our souls and shared our innermost fears, joys, and hatreds. The pieces of my life's puzzle were slowly falling into place.

"I don't understand Duke and his preoccupation with his masculinity when he's really so weak. Why did I feel so lonely even during sexual intercourse with him?"

We talked about it.

"Why don't the men in the engineering offices share technical information with me like they do with each other?"

We talked about it.

"What would happen if the secretaries went on strike? They hold up the whole office where I work. They're the only ones who know anything about the business. Without them, the whole mess would collapse! Yet they do shitwork like serving the men their coffee and get paid shit besides."

We talked about it.

The Thursday night rap groups opened the flood gates of my mind and gave me an education I could have gotten no other way. How I loved those ten women! And how loved I felt.

As I listened and began to see the general picture, how women everywhere were exploited and held back, I felt ready and able to fight back.

Our group went to an underground newspaper and asked to use their mimeograph machine to print leaflets.

Join Woman's Liberation now! Answer the following questions and see if you are sick of being a second-class citizen.

We went by twos, stood on streets in front of shopping centers and supermarkets, and passed them out. Some women would take them and go on their way. Some would say they were not interested.

"It's your life," we reminded them. "Think about it!"

"Go home and take care of your husband and children."

The horse would not drink the water. We learned that the women who needed us would have to find us. We were sad for the women who couldn't look.

I wrote scripts for guerilla theater. On August 26th, the anniversary of the passage of the 19th Amendment, which gave women the right to vote, we performed downtown at the Community Concourse.

It was a great day. We had speakers and women from all over San Diego there to support us. People from the surrounding office buildings came on their lunch hours to watch. Some scoffed and some stayed to cheer.

Colleen was playing the part of a young girl in our skit, and she loved it. My children supported me because they saw what the movement meant to me, but many of my friends thought I had gone mad over this "Women's Lib stuff." I didn't care. My soul had been touched, and I was getting answers to the questions that had bugged me for ten years of sobriety, for all the years of my life. What was most wonderful to me was getting rid of my guilt. I soon realized that my problems weren't unique and even more important, weren't my fault. Women in every culture and of every age shared the same basic frustrations. We were placed on a pedestal, but we ended up as victims. I refused to stick my head in the sand anymore. I wanted to think through every aspect of my life, no matter how much my new insights mocked my crazy past actions. Each insight was a miracle.

Although I began looking for a job again with fresh confidence, there were none to be had. My unemployment ran out. There was no money coming from Karl. The District Attorney? "We're working on it."

All we had to live on was Mary's allotment check. Tim, knowing my dilemma, began sending me money from Vietnam, fifty or a hundred dollars at a time. His sense of humor kept my spirits up.

Dear Nancy & Friends (family included),

This is to inform you...no, that's not right. I'm still kicking.

Your loved ones who are in foreign lands fighting for your freedom and pursuit of happiness, bid you greetings. Please don't worry, Mother. I'm in the best of care that the world can offer. Ta, da-da, da, da, da! The United States Army. Yah, yah, yah. Let's hear it for good old Uncle Sam. Hip, hip, hurrah! Hip, hip, hurrah! Hip, hip, hurrah! Yes, the chance of a lifetime has been laid at your feet. If you're big, dumb or stupid, UNCLE SAM NEEDS YOU! Sam has been looking for a man of your qualifications. Special training will enable you to become the United States Army's greatest weapon. Training starts in two weeks, so be the first on your block to sign up. Remember, it's choice not chance in today's action army. (Specialized individual training for the culturally deprived.)

No, Nancy, I haven't flipped my wig. Just blowing off a little steam. I'm still here with eight months and some days to go. I hope everything's all right back there.

Stay tuned for details.

Who's going to arrest war for disturbing the peace?

Huh? Please may I have a peace?

Another friend kept my spirits up.

Whenever I went out into the backyard and put my hand out, Spot would land on it. I could walk around, and she wouldn't leave. When I hung up the clothes, she fluttered on the line or on a clothespin. I loved her.

I decided to call the zoo, the agricultural department and the college for information. No one knew why a butterfly would do such a thing. They probably didn't believe me. One day Mary took a picture of Spot and me to prove it had happened. I accepted Spot as the reincarnation of Grandma, who I remembered as a closet suffragist.

The one thing I had never wanted to do was go on welfare. I was right. It was the worst spirit-breaking experience of my life.

Welfare sent a social worker to my house to check on the information I had written on the forms a few days earlier. She was pleasant and soft-spoken.

"We can allow you $221 a month for the three children," she said, as if it were good news.

My rent was $165. That left $115 for gas and lights, food, clothes, and anything else, including emergencies.

"How can I live on that?" I asked.

"Well, you could move to another part of town, you know. This is rather an expensive house."

"This was absolutely the cheapest I could find near the children's schools." Couldn't she see the old couch with the springs sticking up?

She went on. "And, of course, you'll have to get rid of that dog."

"Star is my daughter's pet!"

"There are no provisions for a dog that size."

She and welfare can get fucked, I thought.

During the four months we were on welfare, I was depressed. Tim continued to send money. Without that we couldn't have made it. The children did odd jobs for money, and I continued to search for a job. I blamed all our pain on Karl. If only he had been honorable and helped out.

Mary and Susan tried to cheer me up by reminding me of how much better it was now than when I had been drinking. My rap group supported me emotionally, and I never missed a meeting. Tim cheered me up from Vietnam.

Dear Mom,

Please, Mother, don't thank me for anything. Just make sure that you're getting what you need as well as my brothers and sisters. EAT! And don't refuse small favors to my brothers and sisters. That is, a peanut butter and jelly sandwich once in a while. You know what I mean.

Remember the story of the king and the peasant. God would grant favors to the most precious offering given Him. People brought things of all sizes, shapes and values. The people thought surely the king would get God's favor when he set his jewelled crown forward. They were really shocked when the peasant set his three pennies forward for that was all he had. He received the favor from God because he gave his all.

In other words, Mom, don't put your faith in
me to provide, put your faith in your Main Lady.
Peace, Tim

Tim continued to send me money during his entire
tour of duty in Vietnam. No way, at that time, did I feel like
a liberated woman. I begged people for a job. I called all the
places I'd worked before. I went through the yellow pages,
the newspaper, the city, county and federal job files. I was
willing to take anything.

Mary decided to move out. She could live fairly well on
her allotment from Seth, and Matthew's crying settled
down some. They found a place in Ocean Beach, and we all
helped them move.

Then Star ran through the closed patio door.

She had been playing with the kids in the backyard,
happy and running around like a maniac. I guess she
thought the glass patio door was open. It wasn't. Glass
shattered like a bomb. Luckily, Star only got a small gash
on the head, but we had no back door.

I knew the landlord wouldn't pay for it, and I had no
money to get it fixed. The nights were cold. I had to phone
the social worker and beg.

"You understand," she said, "you will definitely have
to get rid of the dog."

I said, "Oh yes, after this, I'll have to."

I lied.

Anyway, I got the money and the door got fixed. Star's
cut healed. My wounds were still bleeding.

I talked to Mary on the phone. "How's the new
apartment?"

"Fine," she said. "How's the peace and quiet at the
yellow house?"

111

"It's okay. We're scraping by on the welfare check."

"Have you been out job-hunting today?"

"What's the use, Mary?"

"How's the book coming?"

"Bad. I can't get into it anymore."

"Boy, Mom, you sound pitiful."

All of a sudden it hit me. I was not going to let the welfare department break my spirit. I had to do something, even if it was the wrong thing.

I phoned welfare and reached a social worker.

"I want you to take me off welfare immediately," I said.

"Just a minute, please." He put me on hold and when he came back to the phone, he said, "You can't do that, Nancy." As if he'd known me all his life.

"I can do anything I want to. And I want to be taken off welfare right now! This minute! My ex-husband should be paying child-support. No one is doing a damned thing about that! The District Attorney's office has been working on it for years."

"I wish you'd think about this."

"I have thought about it, and I'm absolutely sure."

He called me four times that week, trying to get me to change my mind.

"But, Nancy, think of your children. You can't let them go hungry. You must reconsider."

"Look, you. I have exactly five cents in my purse, and I still want you to drop me. Drop me and forget I exist! Your stupid welfare is killing me! Your money isn't enough to live on and yet you call it fraud if I turn someplace else for help. What about the children's father? He's the fraud! You're so afraid I'm going to cheat you, you want me to move my family to the slums and give up everything we've got—including our pet dog. Save your money! And don't call me again! I'd rather starve!"

"I hope you won't regret this, Nancy. We're just trying to help you."

"I'll keep my dignity, thanks. Goodbye!"

Don't tell me about welfare mothers, I thought. Society saw me and the children as losers, not Karl, who had abandoned us. For every dollar they gave us, they took away our independence and pride. If the social worker had known I was taking money from Tim, I would have gone to jail. Yet I never would have survived on welfare without Tim's help.

A day later, I found a job drafting. Maybe because I was angry and aggressive. I had to borrow money from friends because I wouldn't be paid for two weeks, but I was on my way again.

Christmas, the nightmare of poor single mothers.

Steve was working in a gas station, and I wasn't sure how long he would stay in school. To children growing up in a poor family, money seems more important than education.

I was working, but I didn't want any part of the Christmas show. I was determined to buy only small gifts for each child, and Steve did the same. I managed to get enough groceries to fix a dinner, and the day passed happily.

Christmas Day, Mrs. Ellsworth phoned me to tell me Duke had gotten married in Arizona. I was stunned. When I hung up, I felt sick to my stomach. For the first time in thirteen years, I wanted to drink or get some drugs to stop my pain. I couldn't hear anything anyone said to me. I walked around like a zombie.

I finally told Mary.

She said, "Mom, he was probably drunk. You know he loves you."

Why was I clinging to Duke? I had rejected him and gotten him out of my life. Now here I was, feeling rejected. Feeling abandoned again. That no good bastard, I thought. After all I had felt and done for him! And then I heard myself. What had I done? I had used him for a playmate, and now he was playing with some other woman.

Two days later, Duke called me from his wife's house in Arizona. He said he was sitting by the swimming pool and he wanted to tell me the marriage didn't mean a thing.

"I was so drunk, Nancy, I didn't even know what I was doing. Honest, doll, I really love you."

"Don't call me doll!" I screamed. "I'm a woman, not a doll!"

"Okay, okay! Is this more of that women's lib stuff?"

"Yes, and I mean what I'm saying!"

"Okay, I'll write you a letter."

A month later, there was an annulment. Duke had met the woman in an AA meeting. Her husband had divorced her because she couldn't stay sober, and when she and Duke met, they got drunk and got married. Duke had been living in a men's rehabilitation house in Arizona, and I had thought he had a fairly good grip on sobriety for a change. The rich lady had taken him out of the place he was living and married him.

Duke worked as a plumber for a couple of months and then sent me money to fly to Arizona.

I fell for it.

I took a Friday off from work. Duke met me in the airport dressed in cowboy clothes from head to toe. His boots must have cost at least one hundred dollars, and his cowboy hat made him look like the real thing. I wondered if he had a horse parked outside. We grabbed each other and hugged and kissed. He had lost some weight. He really looked good, and I was turned on.

114

We went to a motel where he had rented a room, and he threw me down on the bed. He couldn't get it up no matter how hard he tried. I was totally frustrated and felt like it was my fault. Would I ever get over taking the blame for everything—even a prick?

"I don't know what's wrong with me," he moaned.

"It's okay, honey."

"I guess I'm just too nervous, seeing you and all."

"Let's just sleep. We'll try again in the morning."

Morning came and—nothing. For three days we worked at it, and for three days, nothing. Alcoholism had finally hit Duke where it hurts men the most.

I left on the plane, glad to be sober. Drunk, I had been numb to my feelings. Sober, I could feel joy as well as pain. I wanted to feel all of life. I would tolerate the bad to experience the good.

Tim's letters from Vietnam were full of horror stories about how he'd gotten hooked on drugs, contracted hepatitis and been in the hospital three times. He wanted to come home and straighten out his life.

Dear Mom:

Well, don't ask me what I'm doing here, but I'm writing from the 67th EVAC Hospital. Now don't get upset. I'm not hurt. I've got a bad case of Infectious Hepatitis. No, I didn't get it from dirty needles. The doctor said I got it about four months ago, either from another G.I. or from impure drinking water that the local Vietnamese use. I've been here about twenty-four hours and so far they haven't done a damn thing for me. My stomach hurts like hell. They say I'll see my doctor in the morning. I certainly hope so, I want to get the hell out of here.

It's night and I'm watching the nurses and staff put a patient in restraints. He's got a Bible in his hand and he's flipping out. It's unbelievable. I ask you, what kind of beautiful country is it that forces these young dudes through things like that? I'm sick of thinking about it.

I will write everyday to let you know how I am.

Peace, Tim

"Fighting for peace is like fucking for virginity."

The letters from David were pages and pages of quotes from the Bible, telling me the Word. David was having a good time, and I knew it. But when he started sending me tracts from Moses David, I got disgusted. Moses David was the spiritual leader of the Children of God: unseen, unheard, and hidden away. Was this creep brainwashing the kids and turning them against their parents? I knew David was smart enough to be aware of what was going on. When he figured it out, he would leave. I hoped it would be a good life experience for him.

I always wrote him a return letter and went right along with the whole thing. Once in a while, I would question him. Then I'd get a long letter back. I had no weapon against Bible quotations except my faith in David.

The rambler died while I was still making payments on it to the finance company. I carefully drove the old car to a used-car lot, and there before my eyes was a 1969 442 Olds. It was red with a black vinyl top. I fell in love.

The salesman said the car was in good condition and let me take it for a test drive. The speedometer read 37,000 but I had no idea if they had turned it back or not. I generally didn't trust salesmen, but I liked the car so much; I believed this salesman.

I told him about my loan, and he arranged it so that the loan was paid off and I would make my ninety-dollar payments through the bank. Sold! I gave him one hundred dollars cash, waited for him to do his paper work, and drove away in style. No more station wagon!

An old friend was selling her beautiful eight-foot maple couch. I asked her how much she was asking for it.

"Thirty-five dollars."

"I'll take it."

"But Nancy, it needs re-upholstering."

She hadn't seen my old brown couch lately. "I'll get it re-upholstered with my income tax money."

"Well, I did pay six hundred dollars for it."

"I know. I'm getting a bargain."

My new-found confidence was taking over. I picked out a nice burgundy velvet and left the couch to be redone. I put the ratty old brown one with the springs that stuck everyone in the ass out on the curb for the trash to pick up.

Then the landlord came by to tell me he'd sold the house and I would have to move.

My confidence fell. I cried to Mary again.

"Mom, why don't you move into one of those nice new apartments down the street. You'll have your new couch to put in it, and you can get rid of all the junk you've been hanging onto for years."

"Will they take three children?" I wondered.

"I don't know. Let's go look anyway."

The apartments were brand new and radiantly clean. The walls were white. There was a dishwasher, a garbage disposal, a laundry room for common use and a swimming pool. The two-bedroom unit on the first floor corner was the largest, and way back behind the kitchen was a dining room—a perfect bedroom for Steve.

The white-haired manager said it was $215 a month.

"Do you take children?"

"How old are they?"

"Eighteen, sixteen, and twelve."

"They are almost adults. I'm sure it would be okay."

"How about pets?"

"Oh no, we don't allow pets at all."

I told Colleen the situation and left it up to her. She was truly upset. I let her have some time to think.

"I know we have to move, Mom," she said, coming to me later. "I've been thinking about it. If we sell Star, if somebody pays for her, they'll take better care of her and love her."

"Thank you, honey. I know it was a hard decision."

"I trust you, Mom. I know you wouldn't ask me if you could help it."

I put an ad in the paper, and a couple who already had a doberman bought Star for mating. We all cried when she left.

"At least she'll get to have puppies," Colleen said through her tears.

I had exchanged the family pet for white walls.

The deposit was $100. Steve said, "Don't worry. I'll have a garage sale, and we'll get the money."

Steve labeled every salt and pepper shaker, made signs and drew a big crowd. The junk was on its way out, and he made $165.

I despised moving. I was leaving Spot, who had stayed with me all summer. But the burgundy couch was going to look great against those white walls. It was a new beginning—a red car and a red couch.

Red is for anger.

THE
NEW
APARTMENT

In our new spic-and-span apartment with two bathrooms, I immediately started screaming about how we were going to keep this one clean. No more wet towels left on the bathroom floor! No more dishes stacked in the sink! No more fingerprints on the walls! I almost went as far as to tell the children to take off their shoes before they came in on the beige carpeting.

Steve automatically took his shoes off because of his job in the gas station, but they didn't all work in gas stations.

I was fanatic and happy. I decorated the apartment with my nicest things and spent hours pushing the furniture around until I was satisfied with the arrangement. Then I sat down on my new burgundy couch and looked around.

Eat your heart out, Karl!

Tim didn't pass the urine test for drug use in Vietnam and they were sending him back to the States on a Medi-Vac plane.

The use of drugs in Vietnam had become so widespread that the Army couldn't keep it from the public any longer. They decided to do their own rehabilitating before the relatives of the veterans saw the results of the war with their own eyes. The idea was to send the kids to hospitals within fifty miles of their homes.

Tim was sent to an Army hospital in Fort Polk, Louisiana.

When he phoned, he was mad. "I'm three weeks past time to get out of this fucking army. They've got me in the psycho ward, talking to some dumb shrink."

"I thought you were supposed to be within fifty miles of home!" I protested.

"Tell these bastards that."

"How are you?"

"I'll be fine if and when I ever get home."

"This is insane! Shall I write your commanding officer a letter of protest?"

"Sure, give it a try. I love you, Mom. And I'm all right. Really."

I sat right down and wrote the commanding officer a letter that was so hot it probably burned his fingers. I told him it wasn't up to the United States Army to decide whether or not my son had a drug problem. I told him they had already killed off several thousand young men and now they were tagging those who were lucky enough to escape with their lives, drug addicts. I said my son was twenty-one years old and capable of deciding himself whether or not he had a problem. And if he did, he could handle himself. I said his constitutional rights were being violated and I wanted him released and sent home immediately.

Three days after I sent the letter, I got word from Tim that I could come meet him at the airport the next Saturday.

I stood in the crowd and watched the commercial plane come to a stop. I kept saying over and over to myself, "Thank you, Mother God, for getting him home safe. Thank you. Thank you, thank you, thank you."

Tim was the last person to step out of the plane. He stood at the top of the steps and looked around him like a wary animal. I waved and he started down the steps. His uniform looked two sizes too big for him. The bones of his face were sharp, and there were black circles under his eyes.

I hugged him. There wasn't much to hug. "Welcome home, Tim."

"Yeah, I'm lucky."

We looked at each other and knew what the other was thinking. The stinking, rotten war! Had it been less horrible than a brutal, redneck Texas jail? Probably not. Choose your spot in hell, gentlemen. It's a free country.

On the way home, Tim began to open up. He asked about everybody and told me he would be living with his girlfriend until he got his health back.

"I'm too old to be living with you, Mom. I've got to make it on my own."

"I know it, Tim. Whatever you want to do."

"Do you think Steve and the girls are home? I'd like to see them."

"Sure. Would you like to stay for supper?"

"To tell the truth, Mom, I'd rather party with my friends. I don't want to answer questions or be serious."

What could we do for Tim? Nothing. He was stuck with his memories and his resentment and, like so many other veterans, buried it deep. And I was stuck with "Why didn't I talk him into going to Canada?"

Several days later I received a letter from the Department of the Army, Medical Department Activity, Fort Polk, Louisiana.

Dear Mrs. Hall:

Your son Timothy was transferred to this hospital from Vietnam on 15 August 1971. While a patient in this hospital he was alert, well oriented, showed no signs of thought disorder or psychosis. He was cooperative and his past drug history was considered light.

Your son was retained in the service beyond his discharge date primarily due to scheduling him for air evacuation back to the continental United States. This fact was discussed with your son upon date of discharge from this hospital which was 20 August 1971.

Your son also signed an authorization to remain on active duty beyond his EST until appropriate discharge action could be taken. These administrative procedures were accomplished as soon as practical after arrival at this post.

Information contained in his medical records during his short stay at this hospital and especially his history of light drug abuse, indicates that his home environment will solve the situation.

Please be assured that your son's constitutional rights were not abridged in any way. If I can provide you any further information, don't hesitate to contact this office.

Sincerely,
W.C., Col. MC

Oh, friendly, benign Army, I thought. Gobbledygook to cover your ass.

I owed my endurance through all this to the women in my rap group. They were getting tired, however, of listening to me complain about Karl's not sending child-support.

One night Ruth said to me, "Why don't you forget the money and ask for more pay on your job? You must be worth more than they pay you."

"Of course."

"Well, do it. As long as you keep wasting energy on the money Karl's not sending, you're still emotionally connected with your ex-husband."

"You're right! I'll do it!"

I felt as though a weight had been lifted off me. I began to see myself in a different light. I was an excellent draftswoman, and I worked very hard on the job. I did deserve more money. I knew the men were making more than I was, but I had always accepted the pay difference as part of being a woman in a man's field.

There were only two women in my all-male office: myself and the secretary. The office manager had hired a new man and the secretary leaked information to me that he was making a dollar an hour more than I was, doing exactly the same job. I asked for a raise and didn't get it. I thought about filing a discrimination suit.

Should I or shouldn't I? What if I got fired? I might get black-balled in the industry and never be able to find another job. But if I and other women tolerated such injustice, when would it end?

My supervisor hounded me all day to hurry up and finish my drawing. It was impossible to work any faster, and he knew it. I was filled with resentment. One afternoon, I got up off my drafting stool and told him I had to leave for an hour.

"I have personal business," I told him."

"Right now? What about the drawing?"

"It will have to wait."

"Well, please," he gulped, "come back as soon as you can."

"I will."

I stormed out of the office and down Broadway to the Wage and Hour Board. The officer in charge listened to my story and gave me the forms to fill out for a discrimination suit. He told me they couldn't fire me and the Board would not tell the company who filed the suit until the investigation was over.

"It will take about six months," he said.

"Fine." I felt a tiny surge of power.

I continued to work and watch the investigators come and go each day. The men who had heard me talk about Women's Liberation suspected I had done something, but I never said a word.

The investigators called each man into an office and questioned them about their jobs and salaries. I was called in and asked the same questions.

Six months later, my supervisor called me into his office.

"This is the most ridiculous thing I've ever heard of."

"Justice isn't ridiculous," I told him.

"Well, I don't agree with it at all." He handed me a check for $490. "I have to give you this. It's back pay. You also get a raise."

I thanked him and left. I went back to my drawing board and continued working. By now, everyone in the office knew what had happened. But the secretary was the only person I could rejoice with.

I felt I had won a battle but lost the war. I knew they would be looking for any excuse to fire me. My supervisor began to push me until I had to work three times as hard as everyone else to keep my job. I wouldn't quit. I wouldn't get unemployment unless they fired me.

I hung in there for five months.

I knew in the end they would win. Men play their games for keeps. They may forgive a man for winning but they never forgive a woman. Physically and mentally, I became exhausted.

I had to quit or go crazy.

Looking for a new job, I soon discovered that I had, indeed, been black-balled in the shipbuilding industry in San Diego. I was the crazy women's libber, the trouble-maker, the loud mouth. If I wanted to earn a living, I would have to play the game their way and let myself be underpaid. If I got a job, I would have to keep my mouth shut and take what they handed out. Workers' rights were recognized everywhere in the country. The men had unions. There was no union for women where I worked.

I kept telling myself it had been worth it. I would pay the price so other women drafters or designers coming after me would not have to settle for lower pay ever again.

I had no income at all. I kept in touch with some of the men I had known in the business and found out that a friend had started a business of his own in marine engineering.

I went to his office and applied for a job.

"We'll pay you exactly what we pay the men," he said.

"That's all I ever asked for. And I'll give you my best work."

"We're glad to have you, Nancy."

As I was leaving the office, I paused at the door. "Tell me something, Bill. Did anyone warn you about me?"

He laughed. "Oh yes. Your old boss. He phoned me as soon as he heard I was looking for drafters."

"What did you think?"

"What the hell do I care? We need you. You're hired."

The family cheered, and so did the rap group.

I decided to tell the women about Susan and her problem. They refused to believe that nothing could be done.

Joyce was a lab technician. "I know a really good woman gynecologist who might be able to help," she said.

"You mean you think something can be done?"

"Maybe. Go find out."

The next day I phoned Dr. Rivers and made an appointment.

Dr. Rivers was warm and caring, like no other doctor I'd ever met. She told us there was, indeed, an answer. After Susan finished high school, she wanted to perform an exploratory operation to see just what was going on in Susan's body. Susan agreed.

Susan was in high spirits. She had passed twelfth grade and would be graduating in a few weeks.

The day of graduation, Mary and her children, Tim, Steve, Colleen and I were all there to cheer. It was our fourth graduation. The same school, the same speeches, the same stage and props. But this time it was very special. Susan had known she didn't need the special class. She had known she could finish regular high school. She planned to go on to college. I took everyone to a Mexican restaurant, and we celebrated.

The morning of the operation, I was afraid to ask for time off work. Tim said he would go to the hospital and Dr. Rivers said she would call me at the office as soon as it was over. She said Susan would be groggy most of the day and wouldn't need me. I had taken her to the hospital the night before and stayed to talk to her in case she had any fears. She hadn't been afraid.

Tim called me at the office as soon as Susan came out of the operation and he knew she was okay. Shortly after that, Dr. Rivers phoned me.

"Nancy, she has no uterus. Her appendix was on the left so I removed it. She has four kidneys and no vagina. The operation went very well, and she's fine."

"Wow," I gasped. "It's good you looked."

"Yes, someone might not have diagnosed appendicitis on the left. I'm glad we did the operation."

"'Can you make a vagina for her?"

"She's going to build her own. Doctors used to make an incision, but there is a new method whereby she uses a plastic tube to begin penetration. She's to do this twice a day for fifteen minutes."

"It works?"

"Yes, and later on, she'll be able to lead a normal life."

"I guess, then, it will be important for her to have sexual intercourse on a regular basis."

"You're right. Once she starts having sexual intercourse, it will help keep her vagina open. Or she can go back to doing her exercise."

"Fantastic. I don't know how to thank you, Dr. Rivers."

Right after work, I rushed to the hospital to tell Susan the good news. I apologized for not being with her when she woke up.

"Dr. Rivers was here, Mom. I felt safe."

The apartment that looked so beautiful from the outside was falling apart on the inside. The garbage disposal was defective, and we had to wait for a new one. The windows wouldn't open correctly and the walls were cracking. Ah, new construction.

One day the District Attorney's office phoned and said they had finally nabbed Karl in Florida. He had pleaded poverty in the courtroom but was ordered to pay one hundred and fifty dollars a month for the three children still at home.

The child-suport checks began to arrive, signed by Karl's new wife. Karl celebrated Susan's eighteenth birthday by stopping her fifty dollar payment.

Susan was doing very well building herself a new vagina. Dr. Rivers encouraged and supported her. She listened to everything Susan said and made her feel cared for.

Susan and I decided to celebrate by going ice-skating.

When I was ten, living in Rochester, New York, with my grandfather and grandmother, I put on my first pair of ice skates. By the time I was fourteen, I dreamed of going to the Olympics as a speed skater. My life had squelched that dream.

I discovered I could still skate! I went faster and faster around the rink, feeling the old sense of freedom I'd felt as a girl. It was wonderful. I decided to come skating every week.

That same day, Susan met Marty.

He became her first boyfriend and would share her first sexual experience. Marty was very straight. He had short hair and a bit of a stutter. They fell in love. He courted her for a long time, calling, bringing her flowers, taking her out, and making her happy.

One night when she came home after a date, she said, "Well, it worked."

I knew what she meant, and we both laughed for joy.

In the fall, Susan started classes at the junior college. She wanted to study child development. Suddenly Marty became a born-again Christian. He told Susan they couldn't have sexual intercourse until they were married.

I overheard her talking to Marty on the phone one night.

"Marty, I'm going to school. I don't want to get married yet."

She listened, then answered. "I have to have sex, Marty. The doctor said on a regular basis."

The next time she spoke, she was angry. "Listen, Marty, if God wanted me to be born with a vagina, He would have given me one!"

They broke up, and Susan got deeper into her studies. She was very motivated and determined. I loved to watch her proving her ability. She put me to shame many times.

Steve dropped out of high school in the eleventh grade and was working full time at the gas station, but Colleen had always done very well in school.

One day, at work, I got a call from Colleen's school.

"Mrs. Hall, we have Colleen in the office."

"For what?"

"She was using bad language in her math class, and the teacher sent her to the office. I think she's becoming a behavior problem."

132

"I'll be right there. Don't do anything until I get there."

I drove to the school with my teeth clenched. I walked into the principal's office, well worked up.

"What are you doing now?" I demanded. "I'm not going to let you make Colleen a behavior problem like you did all the others on your tracking system. You've bored them and labeled them for the last time! I'm taking her out of this school right now! For good!"

"Now, Mrs. Hall, just let me tell you what she did."

"I don't care what she did. She's getting all As in her work. She can't be doing much wrong."

"A boy threw her books out the window, and she turned to him and said, 'What did you do that for, you asshole?'"

"Well, wasn't he?"

He looked at me. I dared him to say anything more, with my glare. He put on his glasses and looked at his chart, large squares encased in plastic. Each square represented a class and a teacher.

"She doesn't seem to get along with Mr. Noon, her math teacher. I can put her—let's see—here in Mrs. Long's class."

"Stop!" I shouted. "Stop pointing to those goddamn squares! Is every child in a square? All squared off in little boxes? Why don't you forget that chart and start thinking of children as people and not squares?"

"Now, please, Mrs. Hall."

"Forget it! I'm taking her out of this school for good. Right now! I don't want her to have to go through all the bullshit you put my other children through."

"It's against the law to take her out of school."

"Well, it's against my moral law to leave her in this school."

"I don't think her brothers have anything to do with this. After all, they were different."

"Not in your mind! We're all part of the same family—a broken family. Instead of helping the children, you've done everything you could to make it harder for them."

"I think we can work something out."

"No way. Where's Colleen?"

"In the outer office. I'll get her."

I brushed in front of him. "Come on, Colleen. We're going home. Is that okay with you?"

"Sure, Mom." I could tell by her face she had heard the shouting in the inner office. She was grinning.

The principal continued to talk while we were walking out.

In the car she said, "Am I quitting school?"

"Of course not. We'll find a better school. I've heard about a free school in Ocean Beach. Want to check it out?"

"What does it mean, free?"

"Free of so much discipline and rules."

I wasn't as confident as I pretended. I only knew that I wanted this beautiful young child to have an opportunity to learn in an environment free of labels.

A seed is planted. It peeps through the earth. It grows in its own time until a tiny bud appears. Mother God's sun says, "Reach for me, and I'll give you strength." The bud opens, and suddenly, one day, a perfect flower is blooming, speaking to us all about the joy of living things.

Was my daughter less than a flower?

We drove to the old house in Ocean Beach where the school was held. Inside, we met the young people who ran the school. They were very friendly and informal.

I asked how they managed to keep the kids safe from the truant officer.

"We issue a card for Colleen to carry, stating that she is going to a private school."

"Do you want to try it, Colleen?" I asked.

"Sure!"

The Ocean Beach school had a justice class. All the kids went downtown to sit in on court cases. There was a media class. The kids read and discussed the newspapers. They took nature hikes and learned about survival in the woods, hitch-hiking to Torrey Pines Park and walking the Fat Man's Misery trail.

After a few months, Colleen said she wanted classes with more structure and traditional subjects. I had been investigating the free schools in San Diego and knew there were several alternatives.

Abraxas was an experimental high school run by two progressive school teachers. The tuition was fifteen dollars a month, and the school was located in another old house, this one in Golden Hills, in the heart of San Diego. Abraxas School had regular classes in every subject. The kids could learn at their own pace and didn't have to show up for school if they didn't want to. Colleen missed only three days of school in her three years' attendance.

Abraxas had problems with the establishment. The city closed the Golden Hills school because of a fire law. I thought about all the established school buildings in San Diego that the experts said would collapse in an earthquake. Nobody closed those. Abraxas relocated in a Baptist church on the east side of the city. It took Colleen an hour and a half to get to school on the bus. She had to ride through skid row in downtown San Diego and reported on some of the shocking scenes she witnessed during the bus ride. Most of her homework was done on the bus, however, and she flourished in the free learning environment of the school.

135

I heard a loud knock on my front door one Saturday.

I opened it, and there stood Duke, in cowboy hat and boots, drunk. I wanted to slam the door, but I didn't want him yelling in the hallway of the building, so I let him in.

"I'm all fucked up, Nancy. You wouldn't come to Arizona."

"Please, Duke, get out of here. You're drunk."

"But I love you."

"I don't care, you can't stay. I'll get evicted."

He was sitting and had no intention of going. I tried to get him out of the apartment, to drink coffee, but he said he wanted booze.

"You know I don't have any in the house."

"Drive me to the store."

It was a good way to get him out of the apartment, so I did it. When we pulled up in front of the liquor store, I watched him fumble his way out of the car, and then pulled the door shut and drove away. I left him on the curb, screaming about what a bitch I was.

Before he could make his way back to my apartment he got arrested. Pity was the only feeling I had left for him.

My women's group met at my apartment to plan another march. Two of the college women brought a young man with them to help with the signs and our guerrilla theater. They assured the group that he was on "our side," and we thought we could use him for the part of the male chauvinist in one of our plays.

Carlos loved the part. He was twenty-five and full of fun and wit. We spent three nights rehearsing and making signs. I had never seen a man fit in so well with a group of women.

We performed at the Community Concourse again, and many more women crowded up to see us. They cheered and encouraged us all the way. We felt the change in our audience and anticipated the liberation of women that we believed would change society.

The day after our performance, Carlos phoned. "I'd like to come over and visit you some night, Nancy."

"All right, I'd love it."

After I hung up, I had second thoughts. What did this young student want to visit me, a forty-nine year old woman, for? Who cared? I would enjoy his company.

He arrived that night, all clean and bright and smiling. We had fun talking about the performance, the Women's Movement, the fact that men should start a movement of their own. Suddenly, he reached over on the couch and kissed me. It was a great kiss.

I grinned. "What's this all about?"

"I just think you're a beautiful lady."

I looked at him hard. "Do you want to go to bed?"

He smiled. "You do your thing, and I'll do mine, and if ever we meet it will be beautiful..." he said.

That corny quote broke the tension. In my bedroom, we talked and we kissed, and he told me he wanted to be an actor. We made love all night long with him reciting Shakespeare to me. It was funny but lovely. When I asked why he liked me, he said he couldn't stand the games required in romances with college women.

"I don't want to get involved with heartbreak, and I'm not into marriage. Besides," he said, "I like being with you."

Just after dawn, he got up and dressed, kissed me goodbye, and left.

I lay in bed thinking. Here was a tender, loving man who was not afraid to acknowledge and share his feelings. Why should I reject younger men and restrict myself to men my own age, most of them macho, like Duke. I would

137

probably never see Carlos again, but it *had* been beautiful. I thanked him in my mind for helping to set me free from another meaningless social taboo.

I finished my novel, and my women's group gave a party for me. They made a cake with the title of my book written on it in icing: *Cry Out*. The women made me feel that my victory was their victory.

I found a publisher through the Women's Movement. No male publishing house was interested in a story of a woman's struggle—unless she were a man-worshipping sexpot. But Daughters Press liked it. They wanted to change the title to *A True Story of a Drunken Mother*. It was all right with me.

When the first printed copies of the book came in the mail, I tore open the package and wept. I had been working on this novel for ten years, and finally it had been born. My dream of financial independence had collapsed, however. I got a two-thousand dollar advance and tiny royalty checks every three months. But my novel was on the market. I felt I was reaching out to women all across the country. I began to get letters from readers, warm and intimate letters. I answered each letter with love.

Soon, the pendulum swung back again.

I got laid off and had to sign up for unemployment again. I knew now that I wouldn't make enough from my writing to support us and that I would have to find the energy to both work and write for the rest of my life.

Susan graduated from junior college with a two-year diploma in child development. She found a job at a child

138

care center and wanted to continue in school. She could cover her personal expenses, but her small salary wasn't enough for food and rent.

Steve wanted to move out into a place of his own. Rents were rising and he was looking for roommates to share the cost. The developers in San Diego were having a field day, tearing up the earth and building cheap houses to rent for exorbitant prices. My own rent had gone up to $275 and I knew I would soon have to look for a cheaper place.

One day, while rummaging through my house, I found a small newspaper photo of a Vietnamese woman holding her dead soldier son. I had clipped out the picture while Tim was in Vietnam and forgotten about it. I stared at the woman's face and suddenly decided to paint it. I wanted to capture her expression of screaming rage and horror. I wanted that face to be enlarged, colored in, to remind me and the world of the horror of war.

Could I do it? Could I paint it on a big scale, so that it looked real?

I went out and bought a canvas and oil paints and began.

For six weeks, I worked steadily. I hardly knew anything else was going on. I became the woman I was painting. My desire to make her come alive became a passion. What about her skin color, I agonized. She was an Asian woman. What was the true color of Asian skin? I took a wild guess, or else Mother God directed my mixing of the oils. The color looked right, and I finished my painting.

I couldn't wait for Tim to come over and tell me what he thought.

"Mom, I can't believe you did that."

"What about the skin color?"

"It's perfect. It's a masterpiece, Mom."

Once I thought I would put her in my car and take her to an art show. When I got to the park and saw all the landscapes and seascapes, I decided not to take her out of the back seat.

"Woman-sister, this is not a place for you."

I took her home and put her up on my livingroom wall. She was my first and last oil painting.

I found a job with World Engineering and began to look for a cheaper place to live. The search was discouraging.

The apartment manager was becoming obnoxious. He yelled at all the tenants, especially us, for playing the stereo or for doing anything, it seemed, that humans love to do. I wondered if he was hired to be so cranky and bossy or if he did it because he liked it. Finally Susan told me he hung around the laundry room and bothered the girls whenever they did their wash, pawing them.

"He's a creep, Mom. The sooner we move the better."

I found another apartment in the paper. A two-bedroom for $210. I phoned Tim and Steve to help us move. They gathered their friends together, I bought them a couple of six packs of beer, and we had a hilarious time.

All the way up the stairs of the new apartment, trying to carry the burgundy couch, they yelled at me, "Why didn't you buy a heavier couch? Don't ever move again or you'll have to call Bekins moving company."

APARTMENT NUMBER TWO

Once again we spread out and made ourselves at home in a new place. Colleen and Susan shared a bedroom, and I took the master bedroom for my desk, typewriter, and books.

Tim and Mary were both working at the Waffle Shop in La Jolla. Tim was a short order cook and Mary was a waitress. Tim hated his job. He had started back to college when he got back from Vietnam but couldn't keep up with both job and school.

"When I went in the Army," Tim told me, "they asked me what I did in civilian life. I told them I was a cook. When I got out of the Army and applied for jobs, they asked me what I did in the Army, and I told them I was a cook. It's a conspiracy! I'm a musician!"

"At least now you'll have time for your music when you're off work," I laughed.

"And I'm going to be a musician some day, Mom. You wait."

Steve was working and bought a drum set. He and Tim began practicing and soon had a rock group together. Their music was loud, so they rented a place where they could set up their instruments and play all they wanted to. Then Tim and Mary decided to move in together and they found a huge house in Pacific Beach. The musicians set up in the house.

Mary's boys loved the music. They wanted to grow up to be rock stars too. The house was near where Seth lived, and he tried to take the boys on weekends for brief periods. Tim loved the kids and helped take care of them. So between Tim and Seth, Mary got away once in a while to enjoy herself.

One Sunday, Tim called me on the phone.

"There's something wrong."

"What do you mean?"

"Seth keeps calling here and saying the kids are tired and want to come home. I told him to bring them home, and he said he would wait until Mary got here. So I called Jill's house to tell Mary, and some guy said she wasn't there, that she'd spent last night in jail."

"What?" I gasped. "Where is she now, did he know?"

"Probably on her way home. We'll just have to wait and see."

An hour later, Tim called me back to tell me Mary had just pulled up with the kids in the car. He hung up to check on her.

Two hours later Tim phoned again. His voice was shaking.

"Mom, I don't know what's happening. Mary came in and put the kids in the tub and I asked her about getting arrested. You know me, I said it was no big thing, but I knew she was upset when she asked me if I had told you. When I said I had, she screamed at me. 'It's nobody's business but mine!' That's not like her, Mom."

"No, it isn't. What did you say?"

"I went to my room to play music, and the next thing I knew, the kids were still in the bathtub and she was gone."

"She left the boys in the tub? Oh, Tim, she really is upset."

"Mom," he said, "she called me from a phone booth just before I called you. She was crying. She said she couldn't take it anymore and was turning herself into the hospital."

"What hospital? Why?"

"County Mental Health, Mom. She sounded desperate. I begged her to calm down and come home so we could talk. Mom, I don't know what to do."

My head was spinning. "I'll call the hospital, Tim. You stay with the boys. I'll call right back."

The County Psychiatric Hospital told me Mary had been there and was on her way home. I phoned Tim back and told him.

"She just pulled up, Mom. I'll call you back."

"No, I'll be right over."

I ran to my car and drove down to their house. Mary was sitting on the bed staring into space.

I held her and spoke gently. "Do you want to tell me what happened?"

"No."

"Do you want something to eat? Some coffee or tea?" I motioned to Tim in the doorway. He went for coffee.

"Can't you tell me what happened?"

Her voice was a whisper. "He molested me."

"Who?"

"Doesn't matter."

Tim came back with the coffee mug. I put it in Mary's hand. "Why did they arrest you, Mary?"

"Jill and I were going camping. They stopped me for speeding. Found our beer in the car."

She spoke in a monotone, without emotion. I had to urge her to continue.

"They took me to jail in Vista. They said drunk driving. I was handcuffed behind me. They put me in a van with seven men." A shudder shook the coffee in the mug. She stared at it. "Then a big man in chains. They put him in too. Him. It was him, all the way to San Diego. My blouse. Tore it open. My pants. I kept screaming. They wouldn't stop."

Abruptly, she stopped talking and stared into her coffee cup, not seeing it.

Tim was stomping in the hallway. "Those fucking bastards! Those fucking bastards!"

I tried to get Mary to sip the coffee. Then I left her to call the police. They said they would look into the case. Wildly, I thought of Janet, a therapist in my women's group. I phoned her.

She wanted to talk to Mary, but Mary wouldn't come to the phone. She wouldn't move or answer me. Janet suggested I express my anger in front of Mary. Maybe that would help her express her anger.

I stormed around the room, screaming. It wasn't an act. "Those bastards! Those pigs! Those rotten sadists! They're going to pay for this! We're going to get them for this! Leaving you helpless for thirty miles with that beast! Those fucking, no good, rotten pigs!"

Nothing.

I cried. Tim stormed and cried. Mary didn't move or look at us. I stayed with her until dark, and then went home to call my lawyer, Sherry Van Horn. She told me to bring Mary to her house the next day. I knew it would be a task.

Surprisingly, the next day, Mary agreed to see the woman lawyer. She didn't speak while we drove. At the house, Sherry was wonderfully gentle. She explained to Mary that she wanted to tape the story. She told her we were going to file a suit against the Vista Sheriff's Department.

Patiently, Sherry waited while Mary began her story, broke down, told more, and broke down again.

"Jill and I were camping overnight. I was driving. We had had a couple of beers before we left, and the empty cans were in a trash bag, way in back. There was a six-pack too, unopened. It was late in the afternoon when the Highway Patrol stopped me. They said I was speeding, and when they saw the beer, they arrested me for being drunk. They radioed the Sheriff's Department, and the County Sheriff came. Jill was taken home. They left the car on the road and took me to a county sub-station. I kept telling them I wasn't drunk, that I hadn't had a beer since noon. Jill told them I had two babies waiting for me to come home. I had to wait in the station for the van to transport me back to San Diego County Jail. When it came, they handcuffed me behind my back and put me inside. There were seven men in there. All prisoners."

"Then they brought another prisoner, a big huge man. He was so big and violent they had leg chains on him and chains around his wrists. The chains were about a foot long. They said he had beat up three cops, and they had maced him. The whole van smelled of mace. I was sitting in the front of the van, behind the driver's seat. There was a window between the sheriff and me, but I could hear him talk. I could hear the radio."

"After the van started moving, the violent guy, the man with chains, he made the man next to me change places with him. The other prisoners were afraid of him. I was so scared. I knew it would take an hour to get to the San Diego jail. My hands were behind me. His were just chained together. All over me, his dirty hands were all over me. 'What color are your panties?' he said, pawing me there. He tore my blouse open, pinching my breasts. And other things. I kept screaming and screaming. I knew the Sheriff heard me. I kicked and pounded on the glass with my head. Once he put the chain around my neck. 'This is your last chance before you get to jail with all those lesbos,' he told me. All the way to San Diego I kept screaming and kicking, and that man never stopped molesting me. And the sheriff never stopped. Or looked around."

It's a wonder my moans and groans weren't on the tape of the story.

Mary continued, without animation. "They let me out of jail right away because I wasn't drunk. It was morning and all I could think to do was go back for the car. I hitch-hiked and got a ride. With a nice man. Inside the car, my car, I guess I fainted or something. When I woke up, I decided the next thing I'd better do was kill myself. I started driving in the mountains, thinking I would just hit a tree. After a while, I got to thinking I should maybe go see a psychiatrist first. At the hospital...I guess I went home first. I remember Tim talked to me. I think I saw Seth. Tim or Seth. The psychiatrist told me to take sleeping pills and go to work Monday and try to forget it. the next thing I remember is Mom and Tim screaming..."

After a while, Sherry asked a strange question. "Have you ever been molested before, Mary?"

I was about to protest when Mary looked at me with strange eyes, eyes that said, "I'm sorry, Mother."

She spoke for the tape. "Yes, my father raped me from the time I was seven until I was twelve."

Mother God! My whole body started to shake. No physical pain could equal what I felt at that moment. I tried to control myself.

"Why didn't you tell me?" I gasped.

"You had enough problems trying to stay sober and raise the kids."

I got up and hugged her. We hugged each other and cried.

Karl, the decorated military man, the pride of the Navy. The supposedly healthy one in our marriage. Oh, Mother God, thank you for letting us get away from him.

We drove home in silence, Mary and I, each with our own thoughts. I was thinking about how my gentle, courageous daughter had been assaulted by the male world. What invisible scars would she carry through her life? The police, the protectors of the innocent had let it happen this time. And her own father, for five miserable years, had made her a victim in the meanest way.

And I? I hadn't even known.

Mary remained a walking zombie for a week.

Friends came to see her, to comfort her, to cheer her up. She needed time to bring herself out of the shock of the experience. Her brothers were stunned when they heard about their father. They cursed him in every way they knew.

"I'd like to kill the bastard!" I heard it a dozen times.

I went to my job in a daze. All I could think about was Mary. I hated Karl passionately. I kept imagining the hideous details of Mary's childish helplessness, how horrible it had been for her. I thought about her current boyfriend. Her sexual adjustment must be okay, or she wouldn't deal with him.

A few weeks later, Colleen said, "I want to have sex with my boyfriend."

"You're only fifteen!"

"So?"

I knew she was testing me. I had been conditioned to believe girls should remain virgins until marriage, virgin property for their non-virgin husbands. Why should I support such male-established nonsense? I was trying to raise liberated women.

"You better go to Woman Care, to their group on birth control."

Colleen called and found out when the group met. She rode her bike to the center. She sat in on the group, and when it was over, a woman doctor gave her her first pelvic examination and fitted her with a diaphragm. The doctor left, and two women showed her how to use it. She paid seven dollars and rode her bike home.

"Well, there it is," she said, throwing her new diaphragm down on the coffee table.

"Fine." I didn't know what else to say.

"They said I was too young for birth control pills. Pills upset your body when you're still growing."

"Well, I'm glad you got it all straight."

"I'm spending the night with Jim."

"Oh."

Colleen went about her business, and I was left with my private doubts. Should I have given her a speech about love and togetherness? About sexually transmitted diseases? The schools were doing that. I knew that young women were sexual beings and had sexual feelings at a very early age. I had. No one let me express mine.

I didn't try to stop her from going to Jim's. His mother and father lived in the rich section of the beach area, and Jim had his own living quarters in the garage. His parents seemed to have no problem letting Jim express his sexuality.

The next morning, Colleen came home and said casually, "Is that all there is to it?"

I laughed to myself.

My guilt and suffering over Mary gradually diminished. My daughter became my sister.

No one in the family had enough money to pay Sherry for the paper work and pre-trial expenses. I told our story to the women's group and, little by little, money began to come in from the women of San Diego, who felt Mary's experience could easily have been theirs. The students in women's studies classes took up collections. Some gave a dollar, all they had to spare. It was beautiful.

It took almost four years for the trial to come up.

A few days before the trial date, the judge called Mary into his chambers and said the Sheriff's Department wanted to settle for four thousand dollars. The judge said a trial would be very hard on Mary because it was a civil case, and her entire sex life could be brought into the case. If it had been a criminal case, her private life would not have been relevant to the case.

The judge said the sheriff who had driven the van had been fired, and he, the judge, recommended she settle, for her own sake.

Mary thought about it. She was not ready to cope with a sordid trial. The Sheriff's Department had admitted its guilt, the worst offender had been fired, and perhaps she had gained something for other women with the suit. She settled.

The women's groups in San Diego were going strong. Those of us from the original rap group were facilitating new groups for younger women. I facilitated about four through those years. No dues were charged, no fees were paid. I felt I was giving back what had been given to me, as in AA. Our feeling of connection with the other feminists of the city and state strengthened all of us. The survivors of the world know this need for connection.

One night I was in a group meeting in one of the women's apartments. Suddenly our discussion was interrupted by a high scream from outside.

All seven of us rushed out and looked down from the upstairs balcony. Below, we saw a little girl with a butcher knife stuck in her stomach.

Two of the women were medical technicians and immediately ran downstairs. I called the police ambulance while they removed the knife and administered first aid.

For once, the ambulance arrived in about five minutes and took the girl to the hospital. She lived. The nine-year-old child had been spending the weekend with her father, who lived downstairs. The parents were divorced. Her brother had just returned from Vietnam, and the father left him to babysit his little sister while he went out. The brother had put a pillow over his sister's head and tried to rape her, but she got free and started screaming. He got scared, picked up the butcher knife and stabbed her. Then he ran away. The next morning he turned himself in to the police.

151

After the incident, we could think of nothing else and the meeting broke up. I thought about the two women who had saved the little girl's life but who would never get any medals for it. They had acted quickly and efficiently, without nonsense or hysterics. They made me proud to be a woman.

But who would save the little girl from her memory?

I went out with Duke once in a while, as long as he stayed sober. He had a new car, had passed his contractor's test, and was working for his brother, remodeling houses. He was searching for a woman to take care of him in the traditional way, but I was way beyond that role. He was almost totally impotent because of his drinking. He was getting older and older as I was feeling younger and younger.

The old red car fell apart, and I bought a brand new Oldsmobile, just for me. I continued skating and started taking lessons in figure skating. I started another novel, went to the women's groups, to AA and Narcotics Anonymous meetings. I was making better money these days on the job and was able to dress better, go to plays and concerts, and feel like a human being.

At fifty-two, my sex life was nil. I got into self care. I treated myself regularly to shampoos and hair trims. My hairdresser was one of the new, liberated men—non-macho, gentle and intelligent. He was young and divorced, and we had long conversations about human relationships. He soon became one of my closest male friends.

One day he said casually, "If you ever want to have sex, call me up."

I thought, no, I'd rather keep him as a friend. But he was sexy, and I was horny, and the night came when I made the phone call. He was as good with bodies as he was with hair and conversation.

My children left the apartment.

Colleen graduated from Abraxas, started junior college, and went to work part time at a deli, washing dishes. She had fallen in love with a young man and moved out to live with him.

Steve moved into his own apartment with his girlfriend. Pat was a gorgeous young woman but an addict. She was always stoned. Her family had no idea what to do for her and appreciated Steve's taking care of her. He loved her very much and felt sorry for her. I talked to her, as Steve asked, and even got her to go to a Narcotics Anonymous meeting. The NA group could help her if anything could, but she wasn't ready. It was heartbreaking.

Susan found a better paying job in a dry-cleaning shop and lived in her own apartment. David left the Children of God and was living with some friends and working in a gas station.

On Thanksgiving I resisted the impulse to call the family together for a big dinner. I had given up cooking a long time ago, and my children all had better places to go to celebrate the occasion.

I decided to eat Thanksgiving dinner out and drove past David's gas station to see if he wanted to go with me. He was surprised and pleased and said to pick him up after work.

I went to a movie while I waited. I was experimenting with being alone. I believed half of women's dread of being alone was because they were not used to it. I was right. I was coming to love it, to enjoy a freedom and independence I'd never known.

I took David to one of the most expensive restaurants in San Diego, and we ordered a large meal. We talked and enjoyed ourselves very much. After the dinner, they brought us an after-dinner coffee.

I tasted it and gasped. "Mother God! David, it's booze."

He quickly put his arms around me. "Now, don't panic, Mom. It's okay. You'll be all right."

I gulped some water and sat still. The liquor in the coffee was warm in my stomach. I had not tasted any alcohol for eighteen years, but my memory of it was still green. I knew one drink would lead to another and another, no matter how long I had been sober.

"How do you feel?"

"I think it's all right. Order me some plain coffee, quick."

I was deeply grateful that David took me seriously. He knew that alcohol was a powerful drug to an alcoholic.

The job ended suddenly, and I found myself unemployed.

This time I didn't panic or get depressed. I knew I would find myself another job.

I never felt any loyalty to the companies I worked for. I gave them my best work but not my concern. I had seen too much of corporations. They were all the same, a tight club of competitive boys. They wasted so much money and time that an outsider would never believe it.

Whenever the men in the offices complained about "those people on welfare" I turned red.

"You think you're not on welfare?" I yelled. "Government welfare keeps us all employed here with its contracts. The only difference is this company gets millions and *those* people you're bitching about get a measly hundred."

I kept myself in trouble most of the time, expressing such opinions. The arguments I had were endless.

I got another job. Sandbox, Inc. offered me ten dollars an hour, the most money I had ever earned drafting.

Music was the one thing my entire family couldn't do without. It fed our souls and buffered our pain.

The rock group that Tim and Steve played in practiced long hours and had become good enough to play in clubs around San Diego. The competition in the music industry was fierce, but that didn't stop the group from moving up.

They were asked to play at an outdoor music jam for a Multiple Sclerosis benefit. The whole family showed up for the event, and we had a wonderful day in the California sunshine, listening to the rock music.

Louis Armstrong once said, "There's only two kinds of music: good music and bad music." I agreed and had always liked any good music, whether it was rock, country, classical, musicals, or individual performers. I was proud of my sons.

I was happy to see Tim involved again with his music and succeeding. He hadn't been able to deal completely with his drug problem or his bitterness over Vietnam yet, but I knew he would solve his own problems.

Mary told me that during the first week after she was molested in the police van, when she couldn't sleep, Tim had written and played her a lullaby, singing it to her through the bedroom walls at night.

It was Tim who told me about Steve's lover, Pat.

"She got sick while she was working, the boss told me. You wouldn't believe that bar where she worked, Mom." He shuddered. "The boss told her to go out back to the little house that was there. That's where they found her. Overdosed on heroin. Dead."

Oh, Mother God, sing a lullaby to all the Pats.

I used to drive to work along Mission Bay and dream of living on the water.

I was a single, liberated woman now, with grown children and the nest gloriously empty, but I knew I'd

155

never be able to afford such a place. Only the rich live along the water in San Diego, and the rents were soaring. My own rent had been raised several times and was now $290 a month. Even though I earned a good salary, my plan was always to buy time with my pay and I didn't want to lose that freedom. I needed time away from the eight-hour jail I went to every day. What I really wanted was to crawl into a little hole somewhere and be a writer.

One morning I saw a "For Rent" sign in front of a house on the water. I stopped my car, got out, and a man about fifty-five greeted me. He was warm and friendly. He was wearing a tam.

"What's for rent?" I asked.

"This apartment here. It's $350 a month."

"It's beautiful."

"Gas and lights are included."

My mind started calculating. With the gas and light bills I had been paying, the total would be about the same as I was paying now.

"Has anyone rented it yet?"

"No, do you want to see it?"

It was beautiful. It had a stone fireplace and two bed-rooms. The kitchen was enormous and looked out over the bay, with a view of the city of San Diego. I fell in love with the place and asked him if I could go get my money and make a deposit. He agreed to hold it.

"It's going to be a super place to write," I thought to myself happily, as I drove home for the money.

THE
BEACH
HOUSE

Isettled in the new house, roaming around it like a child with a new toy. This time I decorated for myself. I bought a king-sized bed, a white velvet couch, plants for every corner, and a coffee table made by a Mexican sculptor just for me. I hung my Vietnamese woman above the fireplace.

I was alone. At first, that made me uneasy, but the longer I lived alone, the better I liked it. There were no globs of peanut butter on my kitchen floor. Everywhere around me were expressions of my real self.

I am not afraid of tomorrow
For I have seen yesterday—
And I love today.

I was a sign freak. I loved signs, posters, bumper stickers, and I pasted them up all over my house.

My books were everywhere around me. Since the day I had become sober, I loved books. Often I would stand in the middle of my library and weep, just out of love for my books. All these writers, all these people, believing in something strongly enough to put it down on paper for others to share. The books by women authors were especially precious to me. I could share the experience and feelings of other women. I felt surrounded by friends.

Whenever I got depressed or discouraged with my writing, I would take out a special book: *Child of the Dark* by Carolina Maria de Jesus. It was a cheap paperback of one hundred and fifty-nine pages and had cost me a dollar and fifty cents. It had never made the best-seller list. It was written by a Brazilian woman with a second grade education. It was a story of survival and of keeping three children alive and fed under impossible conditions. With a woman-spirit like Carolina's to serve as inspiration, I thought, no single mother was lost.

At the office they hired a twenty-five year old single mother, new in the engineering business and an excellent designer. She was making about five dollars an hour. We became friends immediately.

"I'm having trouble finding a babysitter for my two little boys," she told me.

"That's the only problem I didn't have when I began working," I told her. "I had so many children, there were always older ones to watch the younger ones."

"How did you do it? I'm having a struggle with just two."

"Have you tried the Senior Citizen's Center? It might be cheaper."

"I'll try there. The best I've found so far is seventy-five dollars a week. It was easier in the winter when the boys were in school part of the day."

"My daughter Mary is having the same problem. She's living at Lake Tahoe now and working as a waitress. Baby-sitters for her two boys eat up her wages."

"I have to be careful around here," she told me. "The boss asked how I thought I could work and take care of the children both. I told him I had to work or go back on welfare. I feel he has his eye on me, waiting for me to make a mistake."

"They never ask the men how they work and take care of their kids, do they?"

I came home from work one day, and my phone was ringing.

It was Karl's new wife. I had heard through his sister that he had married again.

"This is Betty, Karl's wife. I suppose I can get a copy of your book in a porno bookstore."

"What do you mean?"

"Just what I said. It's all lies."

"No, Betty, it's all true."

"Well, if you want to know what I think..."

I hung up. She called back. I hung up. She kept calling and calling, and I kept hanging up. I was getting upset. After an hour, I answered the telephone's ring.

It was Karl. "That book is full of lies."

All my old feelings of terror came rushing back from fifteen years ago, and I felt myself panic, waiting for him to beat me up. Then, I remembered who and what I was.

"That's your opinion, Karl. Actually, you know damn well it's all true. I didn't even include the worst you did."

I remembered what he'd done to Mary.

"I didn't include how you raped your daughter!"

His voice was icy. "What is your definition of rape?"

Mother God! He wanted to discuss semantics!

"You bastard!" I growled. "You're demented!"

I hung up and ignored the ringing of the phone. I was shaking and sobbing and needed support desperately. I called Mary at Lake Tahoe.

"Mary?"

"What's the matter, Mom? Are you crying?"

"Karl and his new wife have read my book. They're really angry. They've been calling and calling and are driving me crazy."

"Do you have his number?"

"Yes." I had it for emergencies. I'd never used it.

"Give it to me. I'll call you back."

161

When Mary called me back, she said she had gotten Karl on the phone and said, "You leave my mother alone. She is a great woman, and you leave her alone."

She said she had heard Betty pick up the extension and knew she was listening, so she spoke to her. "Betty, is he raping your daughters too?"

They both hung up. Karl had married a woman with two little girls. We never heard from them again.

A few weeks later, I was feeling lonesome and horny, and I phoned Duke. The operator came on the line.

"The number you're calling is no longer in service, and there is no new number."

Only a few days earlier, Duke had called me from this number to see how I was. I was surprised, then began to worry. What had happened to him?

I called his mother. She didn't know where he was. I called the police. He hadn't been arrested. I called his brother. Duke had quit remodeling weeks ago. I called AA friends. No word.

I waited for days to hear from him. I got so I couldn't eat or sleep for thinking about him. His family didn't care. Somebody had to care. He wouldn't just disappear without letting me know. We had been friends and lovers for over ten years. I was getting scared and frantic. Should I hire a detective?

I thought about it for a week and finally phoned a detective. It cost me fifty dollars to find out Duke was living with a sixty-year-old woman, in the house she owned.

I laughed, I cried. I wished I had my fifty dollars back.

One of the young engineers at Sandbox, Inc. began getting friendly.

A couple of times each day, he came to my drawing board and began conversations, asking me questions about myself.

I liked him. He had charm and seemed sensitive. He didn't get upset when I expressed my radical views. He seemed genuinely interested.

"Actually, I'm an anarchist," I told him, expecting him to back off. "I don't believe in the state or federal government having control over anybody anymore."

"Does that mean you want to commit violence and overthrow the government?"

I laughed. "No way. I'm for peaceful co-existence. I believe people don't need a lot of laws and controls. They're a lot smarter and more decent than the government gives them credit for. It's the government and the enforcers that commit the crimes of violence."

"But we are the government."

"No way! That's a long-ago dream. Did anybody ask you if you wanted to blow up the world with nuclear bombs? Would you allow chemical wastes to be buried in people's backyards?"

"You have a point."

"The way I see it, the people are left out of all the important decisions. We get discouraged, concentrate on just being comfortable, and hope the so-called leaders know what they're doing. If we weren't so ignorant, if we knew the truth, we'd all be marching in the streets."

One afternoon Frank asked me out to dinner, and I accepted. The talk continued.

"What do you suggest we do about it all?" Frank asked seriously.

I looked at him. "Talking and doing are two different things, I admit. Unfortunately, I have to eat and pay the rent. I really admire the people who try to get out there and do something, don't you?"

"Well, at least you're working on the theory."

"I try to fight in other areas and hold my human self together at the same time. What do you think? Is human-kind going to destroy itself before we do anything?"

"I'm thinking. We're not in a very good field, are we?"

"No. We're just pawns in the war machine. We're not making the bombs or dropping them, but we're helping to install them. I wish I were an expert in some other field. I mean it."

Frank and I became good friends. He was the first man I'd been so serious with, as serious as I was with other women. It was a step. When he fell in love with a woman, later, it was fine with me.

Duke phoned me several times, drunk. The last time, he was hallucinating.

"Hey, Ma. They're killing my ass! Get me out of here! I'm scared."

I hung up, almost in tears. Another man reliving a war of long ago.

My life went on. Writing was my first love, and ice skating was my fun, but once in a while I wanted to get out with people more.

I called an old friend who had been an actress and was now teaching a drama class.

"I think I'll start your class, D.J."

"I've always told you acting would help your writing."

"Well, the truth is I'm scared of it."

"You can do it. Come on down."

I took the class, and it was better for me than therapy. The group was wonderful, and D.J. was a truly great teacher. Before the class, I had only talked and written.

Now I began to comprehend the significance of body language and facial expression. I felt I was growing and learning. That made me feel exuberant, whole and happy.

I went to an AA meeting to share my experience. I loved the anarchy of those meetings. On this visit, I was twenty-one years sober. They gave me a party, and I felt like a real kid.

After the meeting, a gorgeous young man named Eric walked over to me. "Hi, Nancy. Can I talk to you?"

"Sure."

"I have a problem. I really love being sober, but I don't know what to do about my sex life."

I couldn't resist such a straight line. "Do you want to play?"

He looked stunned, then grinned. "Yes."

"Well, I get home from work on Friday at five, so give me a call."

I didn't expect him to call. But if he did, I could use a one-nighter. I planned to work on my book all weekend.

As soon as I walked into the house Friday at five, the phone rang.

"Hi, this is Eric. Do you still want me to come over and play?"

"Sure. I think it would be lovely."

"What time?"

"About eight?"

"I'll see you then, Nancy!"

I showered and stood in front of the mirror. What was I to do about all my wrinkles? Well, what he sees is what he gets, I laughed. They're my wrinkles and I earned them.

When I opened the door at eight, there Eric stood, all shiny clean and smiling. For a moment, we grinned at each other, two shiny people who didn't know what to do next. We had coffee, talked and began to feel more comfortable. Soon, he kissed me and we made love. In bed, we smoked and laughed and played some more. At one point, I got up and went to the bathroom. When I looked in the mirror, I screamed.

"Damn, I'm getting old!"

Eric came into the bathroom, took hold of me, and laughed.

"You're funny."

"Do you know how old I am? I'm fifty-five!"

"I'm thirty-one. So what?"

"Skin is only one organ of the body," said Eric. "The soul is much more important, and you have a beautiful soul."

Eric was starting a new life at that time. He wanted to be a doctor. He lived with a roommate and studied very hard. We saw each other on weekends and committed ourselves to each other for just one day at a time—which is all anyone can do.

There were protests and rallies going on against registration for the draft. I joined the Committee Against Registration and the Draft and passed out CARD leaflets in front of the Post Office to the young men who were going in to register.

A protest was planned for Monday at the University of California, San Diego, but I had to work. Eric said he would go alone and march. I got in my car Monday morning to drive to work, but halfway there I stopped. I couldn't stand it. I had to go to the protest.

I went home, put on my jeans and t-shirt that said "Resist the Draft" and drove to the university. I was sitting on the ground, listening to David Harris speak, when I heard Eric speak from behind me.

"Nancy, I thought you went to work."

"I couldn't. I just couldn't."

"You're funny."

He didn't understand my history. He didn't know how many times I had put my job before my convictions. It was time to reverse my priorities. I wanted to march against war.

We marched together.

The contract was not renewed at Sandbox, Inc., and I was laid off March 2, 1980. I signed up for unemployment and began some serious work on my book.

On May 24th I woke up in the morning with double vision. I thought it would go away, that I had been using my eyes too much. I waited and it didn't go away.

Colleen had moved back in with me, so I wasn't alone. I finally decided to go to my doctor. He gave me some coordination tests and took blood tests and said he couldn't find anything wrong with me.

I went back a second time, and he referred me to a neurologist, a Dr. Frankenstein. He did the same coordination tests and sent me to a lab for blood tests. He said to come back in two weeks if I wasn't any better and charged me $60, which I paid in cash so I wouldn't run up any bills.

My eyes got no better. I couldn't write. I couldn't read, and I sure couldn't go to work. I returned to Dr. Frankenstein in one week, and he gave me a tensilon test. I had no idea what it was for, but it didn't help. I was to return in two weeks if I wasn't better.

My money was going fast, and I had to switch from unemployment to disability. I was getting calls from corporations to go back to work, and I had to refuse. My bills were going unpaid, and the dunning notices were coming in.

"I'm trying to tell you I'm doing what I can!" I screamed. I was scared.

On the 19th of June, I returned to Dr. Frankenstein. He said he wanted me to take Decadron, that it would fix my eyes.

"I'm a sober alcoholic," I told him. "I haven't taken drugs or put anything toxic in my body for twenty-two years, and I'm not sure I should take this. What is it?

"It's cortisone. It's not a drug. It's an anti-inflammatory medication. It will cure your eyes."

I paid cash for the visit and drove to the drugstore to get the prescription filled. Luckily, it wasn't far. I could drive all right if I held my head to one side to see.

The druggist's daughter had gone to Abraxas with Colleen. "This is pretty strong stuff, Nancy. You better be careful."

"But the doctor prescribed it, Joe, and he's one of the most respected in San Diego. I don't know what else to do. I have to get my eyes straightened out."

I was to take four pills a day for ten days. I checked at the library. According to the Physicians' Desk Reference, that was the second strongest dosage of cortisone used. I wondered if Dr. Frankenstein had read the Reference lately.

I expected to get better long before the ten days were up. I kept myself busy playing albums, taping music I liked from the sixties, talking on the phone, and lying in the sun. On the fourth day, I started to feel strange. I got very thirsty and couldn't seem to get enough liquids down me. Eric and Colleen kept getting me cokes, and when they were at work, a friend brought in more cokes. She fixed me food and tried to take care of me.

"I think I'm getting worse," I told her.

I asked Eric to take me to a CARD meeting. "I have to be where there's political action going on," I said.

"You're getting delirious, Nancy. And you look as if you're losing a lot of weight."

"I'll be all right. Go about your business."

Tim and Steve came by to check on me. They fixed me smoothies. Everyone seemed to know what I needed, and no one thought I was dying—not even me.

I lost twenty pounds in five days. I couldn't eat and I couldn't go to the bathroom. I had thrush mouth and vaginitis. Every time I called Dr. Frankenstein, he told me I'd be all right. He ordered medicine for my mouth.

One morning, when everyone was gone, I decided to go to his office and show him what I looked like. How I made it there, I'll never know. I drove very slowly, parked the car, and stood in his office. He came out and stood behind the counter.

"Look at me! Look at my mouth!" I slurred.

"Well, you'll have to go down the hall and see the dermatologist."

"I can't see to fill out another financial statement," I protested.

"My secretary will give you a xerox copy."

I had to hang onto the wall all the way down the hall until I finally saw the number on the door. I went into the office. There were three people ahead of me.

When I finally got in to see him, he said, "Oh yes, typical case of thrush mouth. Here's a prescription for vaginal suppositories. Use one every six hours."

I made it home. If I had been stopped by the police, I would have been arrested for being drunk and died in jail.

On July 3rd, I called a friend and asked her to drive me back to Dr. Frankenstein's office. This time I had someone with me in the office.

"I've lost twenty pounds and I'm very sick."

"Well, you'll have to see an internist. I'm a brain surgeon."

"No, that's it! No more doctors!"

My friend spoke up. "Are you just going to wash your hands of her?"

169

The doctor gave us an arrogant look and turned away. We went home.

"Nancy," my friend said. "Some of your symptoms are serious. And you're miserable. That doctor is irresponsible!"

On the eighth day, I threw out the pills. I was lying on the couch, and Eric was trying to comfort me. I was extremely embarrassed because I looked like a POW and didn't want him to see me that way. I looked out at the tree. The leaves were fluttering.

"Eric, the leaves are calling to me to come out and play."

He felt my forehead. "Do you feel feverish?"

"I feel like going out in the middle of Emerald Bay. I have to get that icy water in my blood."

"Honey, do you want to go to the hospital?"

"No, I want to go out in the middle of the bay."

Fourth of July came and with it the fireworks over the bay. I stayed on the couch, holding my cold can of coke. I had told the rest of the family to go watch the fireworks, that I would rather be alone. I stared into nothingness, not seeing, seeing...

I walked straight and tall into a roomful of women. It was the room in *Midnight Express*, except that the women were all walking around the pole in one direction. In the center was a man in a suit of armor, sitting in a chair, directing them. They were all the women I had ever known—my sisters.

Suddenly I was yelling. "Stop! Stop right now! Leave! Go! You don't have to do this!"

The women all ran up to me, hugged me, and started to leave.

There was no face on the man. I walked up to him, bent down, and looked at the closed armored face-plate. I put my face close to the plate. Suddenly it flew open, dropping from the top. Gallons of blood rushed out at me.

The morning of July 5th, Eric and Colleen took me to the hospital. I went into ketoacidosis and coma. I had a blood sugar level of 777 by the time they checked me.

When I came to my senses, I vaguely remembered them trying to shut me up. I must have been doing a lot of screaming. When I realized that I was in a place where people were dying, I felt terrible that I had made so much racket. The nurses said I had screamed at the doctor on duty who was trying to save my life. I apologized and told them I had been unaware of it. That didn't seem to make any difference.

I thought to myself, "Next time I'm in a diabetic shock, I'll try to mind my manners."

In the intensive care unit, each patient had a nurse. The first nurse assigned to me was cold and unfriendly. She seemed annoyed every time I asked for a bedpan. Finally I kept the bedpan on the little table beside my bed, the same table they put my food on. The nurse would empty it and put it back. I didn't get my sheets changed or my body washed. It seemed strange.

No one talked in that place of death. In desperation, I caught the eye of the man at the command center and motioned him to me.

"Do you think I could have a piece of paper and a pencil?" I whispered. "I'm a writer, and I would like to write."

"You should sleep. It's three in the morning." He spoke in a soothing voice.

"Please," I begged. I didn't want to sleep. I kept fighting to stay awake. I had a deep dread of sleep, I don't know why. My legs ached constantly.

"Okay," he said. "I'll see what I can do."

I lay there, afraid that he too would ignore me, but he returned in a few minutes with a pad and a pencil. He was grinning. "Is this what you want?"

He was right to grin. I was too sick to write. I hugged the pad and pencil to my breast like a teddybear.

The next day, Tim and Steve and Colleen came to visit me, one at a time and only for a few minutes. Eric wasn't allowed in because he wasn't one of the family. The children kissed me, told me I was going to be all right, and that I was too tough to die. Laughing made me feel like a human being again.

The phone kept ringing at the command center—Chris from Santa Cruz, Mary from Lake Tahoe, David from Portland, Oregon, and Susan from Texas, where she was living with her new husband. Each wanted to know how I was coming along, and I overheard the nurses say, "She's stable now."

Later that day, Dr. Frankenstein appeared at the foot of my bed. I was shocked that he had bothered and I didn't want him near me.

"You're going to be all right."

No thanks to you, I thought. I stared at him.

"Well, at least your eyes will heal up now."

Cute. I couldn't believe my ears. I continued to stare, too sick to argue with him, and he left. Later, he claimed to have examined me during this two-minute visit. He wouldn't have dared. I probably would have tried to punch him out if he had come close to me.

He was the only doctor I remember coming to see me while I was in intensive care. Lying there in my bed, weak and vulnerable, I couldn't help noticing the difference between the care and comfort given the other patients by the nurses and the minimal care given by most of the doctors.

In a bed not far from me, an old woman lay dying. Her doctor came to check on her once. He walked into the room in tennis shorts and shoes. He put a white coat on over his playtogs before he went to the woman's bedside, stayed only a minute, and left hurriedly for his tennis game. The woman died that same afternoon, and they wheeled her out. I imagined what his bill would be for services rendered and, in my mind, compared it to the pay of the nurses, who had truly tried to make her last moments comfortable.

On the third day a new nurse came on duty. She was a woman about my age. Her voice was cheerful and her smile was warm. What a difference her humanity made in that dismal place!

"Let's see if I can't get you cleaned up this morning. How about a nice bath?"

"I could sure use a bath."

She bathed me all over with tender, caring hands. While she changed my sheets, I asked her how long she had been a nurse.

"Twenty years," she said proudly.

"Nurses don't make enough money for all they do," I said.

She laughed. "No, and there's not enough nurses to go around because of it."

"What keeps you so cheerful and caring in spite of the overwork and low pay?"

"And arrogance of doctors," she added. "Well, I figure sick people are still people, and they need a lot of TLC. They didn't ask to come here or feel so miserable."

"Well, I tell you, you've brought a lot of sunshine into my life today!"

I began bugging everybody about getting out of intensive care and into a room. My legs were still hurting, but I was feeling better. They told me when the last bottle of saline was finished, I would be moved to a room. I had watched five bottles of saline drip, drip, drip into my arm.

As soon as I was moved, I asked for a pencil and a piece of cardboard. I made a sign and stuck it over my bed.

NURSES NEED
MORE MONEY!

The nurses loved it. Nurses and secretaries—they hold up the world.

I had a phone in my private room. I always felt safe with a phone. But instead of my calling other people, people called me. All my friends and two of my former employers. I was feeling like myself again.

Almost immediately, I began to worry about money. Who was going to pay the hospital bill? Colleen and Eric had pooled fifty-two dollars to get me admitted. Without that, would the hospital have turned me away? I was completely out of money, having used all my savings on the doctors' bills.

Then somebody, somewhere, punched the big computer and found out I was unemployed. Two ladies came to my room to take down information so that Medi-Cal could pay the bill. The personal questions they asked me made me feel like an indigent.

Finally one of the women said, "The total cost is $3010, and you will be expected to pay some of that. We don't know how much yet. Your doctor wants you to go home tomorrow."

"Tomorrow!" I gasped. "I can hardly stand up to go to the bathroom!"

"You'll have to discuss that with him."

When they had gone, I thought about the old people who couldn't fight for themselves, who had to endure humiliation because they had no money. How many of them were turned out of the hospital when they still needed medical care?

The next day a doctor I had never seen before strode aggressively into my room and perched himself, half sitting, on the sink. He was quite young. I figured he was the man who had saved my life, but before I could thank him, he curtly dropped a bomb on me.

"You have diabetes and will have to take insulin the rest of your life."

Was he still angry with me or was his bedside manner always this bad, I wondered. I refused to give him satisfaction.

"So what?" I said. "I've been through a hell of a lot worse than that."

His face looked blank.

"Next statement please," I said.

"I'm releasing you today. I want you to come to my office this afternoon at four to get a prescription."

Why don't you give it to me now and save me the trip? I thought. I didn't say it aloud and wished I had. I thought I knew the answer: he wanted to be able to charge me, or Medi-Cal, for an office call.

I phoned Colleen, and she said she would come pick me up. I said goodbye to the nurses.

"We're sorry to see you and your sign go, Nancy. Good luck."

We stopped at the doctor's office and I found out why he had wanted me to come by. He took me into a closed office.

"Don't ever take cortisone again, Mrs. Hall."

"Was the cortisone what made me sick?"

"You had an extremely high blood sugar level. They don't mix."

"Wouldn't that have shown up on the blood tests Dr. Frankenstein took?" I looked at his non-committed, blank face and knew the answer. "He didn't read my blood tests, did he?"

He nodded. "Do you eat a lot of sweets?"

"I'm a sober alcoholic. I love sweets."

"Too much sugar makes anyone susceptible to diabetes."

I stared at him and knew he wouldn't give me any more answers. I knew he was trying to protect Dr. Frankenstein, who had been guilty of the grossest carelessness: not reading a blood test, giving cortisone to a patient with a very high blood sugar level, and repeatedly ignoring the danger signs as that patient slowly went into diabetic shock and coma.

I repeated the conversation to Colleen, wondering if an objective person would draw the same conclusions. She did.

"Wow! Wow!" she said. "That's malpractice if I ever heard of it!"

"It's worse than human error, isn't it?"

"It's gross. He wasn't paying any attention to you at all."

I sighed. "I'm lucky to be alive, Colleen. Just take me home."

Someone had made arrangements for a nurse to come to my house the following day to show me how to use insulin. She also helped me plan and measure my food intake. I told her what the doctor had said about taking insulin for the rest of my life.

"You don't have diabetes, Nancy," she said. "You have temporary steroid diabetes. You'll be off the insulin in a couple of months."

I was shocked and delighted. "Fantastic! I wondered because there's no diabetes in my family. Why did the doctor tell me that?"

She rolled her eyes. "Just find a doctor who will keep track of your blood sugar for you. And stay on your diet. The American Diabetes Association will send you some literature."

I went to five different doctors before I found one who would listen to me. I got off the insulin, stayed on my diet, and went back to work in September.

I was thin and weak, but I had made up my mind to get well and stay well. No more doctors! I read books on nutrition and figured out what my body needed. I took vitamin supplements and analyzed what I was lacking.

My eyes healed, and I talked to a lawyer.

"If you had died, Nancy," he told me, "your children would be very rich. Or if you had been blinded or had lost a limb, you would win a malpractice suit easily. But there are so many cases worse than yours, your experience looks like a picnic."

"What do you think then?"

"A near-death experience is not funny. We're going to sue."

"Will the court be sympathetic? How will they view me?"

The lawyer grinned and handed me the hospital medical report that the doctor had made out on July 5th. It read:

> Nancy is a 57-year old confused white woman who presented to the Emergency Room with increasing confusion, approximately a 20-pound weight loss, and polydipsia. On interviewing Mrs. Hall, the history that we are able to obtain is very unreliable because of her confused mental status. However, as best I can tell, she has been under the care of Dr. J. Frankenstein because of some diplopia, and a fourth nerve palsy (history given by Dr. Frankenstein). After being seen by Dr. Frankenstein, she underwent a diagnostic work-up which apparently included, but wasn't limited to a tensilon test. Apparently, Mrs. Hall was administered systemic corticosteroid, and shortly thereafter began becoming increasingly weak

having increasing weight loss (approximately 20 lbs. over three weeks) and became increasingly thirsty and polyuric. Because of the above noted complaints, she apparently found her way to the Medical Center E.R. where after a brief evaluation was admitted. I questioned Mrs. Hall regarding the past medical history of diabetes is (sic) unrewarding. Specifically, the patient states that she has never been told that she was a diabetic in the past, and to the best of her knowledge has no family history of diabetes. The only significant past medical history that we can elicit from Mrs. Hall is the fact that she is a "reformed alcoholic" and states that she hasn't touched any other drugs that she uses on a chronic basis and similarly denies ever having been told of any serious medical illness in the past....Social history is significant in the fact that she is divorced and has raised several children, none of whom apparently are living with her at the present time. We were unable to elicit any other significant history because of her altered mental status.

I looked up at my lawyer's grinning face.

"Wow," I shuddered. "It makes me sound like a crazy derelict. And I don't remember any of it, the questions or the answers. He didn't believe anything good about me, did he?"

"I doubt it," said the lawyer. "But so many of them— the doctors, their families and friends—drink or pop pills or use drugs that they don't believe for a minute there are sober people in their care."

"And what about this social history? It implies that none of the children can stand to live at home with me."

"That's right. The medical establishment sees you as an ex-drunk, divorced, crazy lady who probably pops pills and won't admit it, claiming righteousness in sobriety."

"I don't feel righteous." I shivered. "Could I have a copy of this report to show my family and friends? They'll never believe the cold-bloodedness of this picture."

He gave me a copy and shook my hand.

"We go to trial in 1983, Nancy."

I was fifty-eight years old, and for the first time in my life, I was physically tired.

When I first came home from the hospital, I had been afraid to sleep in the bedroom, in the bed where I had almost died. After three nights of sleeping on the couch, I moved the bedroom furniture all around so I could stand sleeping in the room.

While I was sick, I was like a wounded animal, wanting to be left alone. While I was getting well, I needed to be independent. Eric encouraged me and loved me and, having gone through the entire experience with me, was determined more than ever to be a good doctor.

One day Colleen put an album on the stereo: "Easy to Be Hard" from *Hair*.

"I played it every day you were in the hospital," she said.

I couldn't hold back the tears.

I went back to work at Sandbox, Inc. in September and got laid off in January. Their contract was not renewed. I found another job in March. It was a new company, and I was one of the first to be hired. It looked as if this company would be in business for a long time, and I felt I had finally found a home. The environment was great, but I was still making drawings for the Navy.

I continued to go to CARD meetings and keep up my faith in the grassroots efforts to solve the political situation. Eric had taken a political science course and was becoming politically active.

Mary Daly came to San Diego, and I asked Eric if he wanted to go with me to hear her speak about women and religion. He went, and he loved it. That evening I met and talked to my feminist sisters of San Diego, some of whom I hadn't seen for ten years. I couldn't help thinking I might not have been there. Listening to Mary Daly speak, I thought of my own Higher Power, the Mother God, the Creative Force that had kept me alive. I could not fathom the father God. My spirit had been fed by women. Women, the creators, not the destroyers of life. Was it the father God image in men's minds that allowed them to seek power over cooperation, profit over fulfillment, death and destruction over life and joy? When would the Mother God, the earth, and life become society's first priority?

In June, my drama teacher, D.J., phoned me.

"Nancy, we're going to do a benefit for the Battered Women's Center. With all the cuts in the government budget, they need money. I want you to read a scene out of your book. Will you do it?"

"Sure! Who's going to be in it?"

"Some of the women in my classes and a lot of professional actresses."

"Do you want me to pick my own scene from the book?"

"Absolutely. You know what would be best. Our first rehearsal is Wednesday night."

"Okay, I'll be there."

We called it "A Woman's Celebration," and it was exactly that! Sixty women showed up—beginning actresses and several professionals from the stage and television. We planned about twenty-five different scenes, from plays, poems, and monologues about women. I had picked a beating scene from my book and was to be the final woman to go on stage. The program touched on every facet of women's lives: comedy, tragedy, love, sex, and dreams. My reading brought the program around full circle. I wore black.

Backstage, we became sisters immediately. We shared life stories. Some of them weren't very pretty. Much of our warmth and intimacy came from the knowledge that we were all doing something for women who couldn't help themselves.

One of the women was separated from her husband, who thought that being in such a performance was the silliest thing he had ever heard of. He came to one rehearsal and then to both performances. He came backstage afterwards and told us he had never known what women went through. That night, he and his wife got back together.

We had three rehearsals. During the entire time, including the performances, there was not a fight or an ounce of jealousy. I had never witnessed so much cooperation and support in my life. There were 73 women in the group.

The night of the performances, everything had to go like clockwork. We had to move fast to get the twenty-five skits done in the allotted time. Tension was high. One actress had her nose broken by her partner's elbow as they were rushing to leave the stage after their scene. Two other women rushed her to the hospital, where the doctors wanted to make out a police report. They thought she was a battered woman.

Two battered women from the Center came to the performance. They rode to the theatre in the trunk of a car because their men were still looking for them.

"A Woman's Celebration" brought in a thousand dollars for the Battered Women's Center.

I was elated. I was triumphant. I was bone-deep tired.

I told myself, "Give yourself a break, Nancy. You nearly died less than a year ago. You're just now getting your weight back up." I felt like Gertrude Stein when she said, "I think I'd like to go to bed for four years."

I got home from work one day just in time to answer the ringing phone. It was Mary.

"Hi, Mom. I just called to tell you I got hit by a train and I'm okay."

"You're kidding me!"

"No! We went to the desert camping, and on the way back, we had to cross an old railroad track. The sage brush was so high, we didn't see this slow train coming and it hit us. It didn't do anything but dent the car and shake us up though."

I could not stop laughing. "I don't want to hear it. I've had all the train wrecks I can handle in one lifetime."

On the other end of the wire, Mary laughed with me. "Otherwise we're fine," she added, and we laughed more.

Mary was her old self. Mother God be praised.

My finances had returned to the even mark and I was anticipating saving a little money. With Reagan and the Congress tampering with the Social Security system, I began to think I would have to keep sitting at my drafting board long after 65 to survive.

It was getting more and more difficult to drag into work every day. I had two male friends there who had been activists in the sixties when I had first known them. Now, like me, they were working in the world of technology, disliking their necessary but compromising situation. We agreed on every political issue except sexism. They couldn't comprehend or sympathize with the issues.

"I agree with equal pay for equal work," they said.

"But how do you feel about a secretary's experience counting toward seniority in management?"

"Well, it's not the same, of course."

"What about the issue of child care being provided? Isn't the raising and care of children a social issue?"

"Once they get to school age, there's no problem."

"Don't you see that abortion must be paid for by Medicare, or non-privileged women are barred from it?"

"I figure if a woman won't take the pill, it's not up to society to bail her out when she gets pregnant."

It was hopeless. Every sane bit of progressive thinking we had done in the sixties was ended. Our dream of a more human world had stopped with the obvious issues: ending war and letting the blacks vote in the South. We had only begun to change things, and people were already tired of thinking. We were handing everything back to that self-righteous, simplistic bunch called the Moral Majority and to the ruling class whose only god was money. The media was playing games with the news, implying that violence was the result of not enough law and order. The this-is-the-answer experts were getting rich with faddish and trivial advice.

I began to sink deeper and deeper into depression.

I kept it to myself and tried to act normal with Eric and Colleen and all my friends. I shuddered when I heard people say, "The Women's Movement has topped out and is over." I wasn't positive they were wrong.

I decided to commit suicide, to end it all.

Before I could perform my last act, there were several things I had to do.

First I had to find my will. With all the drama I could muster up as inspiration, I started to go through my filing cabinet and all my papers. I cleaned out my desk, my closet, my boxes of writings, and threw out things I had been keeping for years.

When I was just about through it all, I found my will in the bottom of a drawer. I read it and was very pleased. There would be enough insurance money for each of the children to get a few thousand dollars. That would help them for a while.

"Why haven't I been able to make more money in my lifetime?" I asked myself.

Second, I tried to finish my book. I couldn't write, and I became so traumatized that my blood sugar went up again. Did I have to go see a doctor? Yes, I had to get fixed up until I finished organizing my life. The doctor prescribed sixteen dollars worth of pills for diabetes, and I took them.

What about Dr. Frankenstein and his self-protecting gang at the AMA? I decided they weren't worth bothering with.

My unfinished book was worth bothering about, and I was in agony over abandoning it. Was I going to forget all about single mothers? About my sisters?

"They will be okay," I told myself.

Colleen walked into my bedroom.

"Hi, Nancy. What are you doing?"

"Sitting."

"You know, Nancy, there's something I've been wanting to tell you for a long time."

"Yeah?"

"It's about my childhood."

"Oh no, I can't handle it."

"No, really. Listen, will you?"

"So?"

"I've been doing some thinking lately. I had the greatest childhood of anyone I know. I love this paradise I've always lived in. I love Mission Beach, the little shops, the people, the nooks and crannies. I loved all our houses. I loved Tim's and Steve's rock-and-roll band, all the music we've always had in our house. All the love we've always had in our house."

I gulped and tried to hold back the tears. Colleen didn't know I was planning suicide.

"But what about Duke and Karl and the drinking and the drugs and all that?"

"We always trusted you because you were sober. That made us feel secure. We always knew that anything you did was okay."

"That's the nicest thing that anyone has ever said to me."

"I just wanted to tell you."

She left and went about her business.

I decided I wouldn't end it all until I finished my book. Page by page I began to feel better.

I got a call from a company that was not in the shipbuilding business. They offered me a job, and I said I could start in two weeks.

I phoned the doctor who had given me the pills.

"I just threw out the pills, Doc. Fuck pills! I'm going to stay well and live!"

Well, here I go again. There would be more problems, more layoffs, more love trouble and car trouble and house trouble, and no money—but so what?

The phone rang.

"Hi, Nancy. This is Liz. The Women for Peace are marching Saturday against U.S. involvement in El Salvador. Do you want to come?"

"I sure as hell do!"